BUSINESS UNLOCKED

From Startup to Success : Unleashing Your Entrepreneurial Potential

Anuj Sharma

Copyright © 2023 Anuj Sharma

Business Unlocked Book

CONTENTS

FREE BONUS

Exclusive Bonus Offer for Business Unlocked Book Owners!

Hey there, valued reader! I want to express my heartfelt appreciation for purchasing this Book. As a way of saying thank you, I have an exclusive bonus package that will take your business journey to the next level!

To claim your bonuses, simply visit this page https:// rcl.ink/6vEFG . Once there, you'll gain access to an incredible set of six Business Worksheets designed to provide you with practical guidance and help you unlock your business's full potential.

Here's a sneak peek of what you can expect from these powerful worksheets:

1. Find Your WHY Worksheet: Uncover the deep inner purpose of your business, helping you align your values and mission to drive meaningful success.

2. Competition Research Worksheet: Analyze your competition and improve your positioning in the market, giving you the competitive edge you need to

stand out.

3. Customer Avatar Worksheet: Clearly define who your customer is, allowing you to effectively tailor your marketing efforts and connect with your ideal audience.

4. Goal Setting Worksheet: Set and achieve your goals easily and efficiently, ensuring you stay focused and make tangible progress towards your business objectives.

5. Problem Solving Analysis Worksheet: Develop critical thinking skills to address and resolve business problems, empowering you to achieve high growth and overcome obstacles.

6. Product Demand Analysis Worksheet: Evaluate the demand for your new product or service before launching, enabling you to make informed decisions and minimize risks.

To access these resources, simply visit https://rcl.ink/6vEFG

Also, another exclusive bonus is waiting for you on the Last Chapter of this book.

INTRODUCTION

Do you know that 1 in 5 Businesses fail in the 1st year, according to the U.S. Bureau of Labor Statistics (BLS).

If like me, you want your business to thrive for many years to come. I suggest you read this book till the end.

Welcome to the 'Business Unlocked' book. I am Anuj Sharma and just like you even I was struggling with my business once. With time and hard effort, I learned the proper ways to run a business and overcome various business problems.

I have been fortunate to help many individuals achieve success in their respective businesses.

This book, 'Business Unlocked' is one of my attempts to share my knowledge with you with the hope that I will be able to provide you with the basics and fundamentals of running a business that we as business owners don't tend to think much about, till the problems start to grow and make it uncomfortable to operate our business.

'Business Unlocked' is a comprehensive guide to improving the performance and profitability of your business. This book offers practical, actionable advice on a wide range of topics, including marketing, finance, operations, etc.

Whether you are a small business owner or a corporate executive, this book provides the tools and techniques you need to drive success in today's fast-paced, competitive marketplace.

'Business Unlocked' is an essential resource for anyone looking to take their business to the next level.

This book will help you to:

1) Prevent failures in your business.

2) Increase your sales.

3) Make more money.

4) Build a great team around you.

5) Build a great company.

6) Turn around your business from failure to success.

7) Create a great brand.

8) Get more customers.

9) Get more sales.

10) Make your business grow faster and bigger.

11) Systemize your business.

12) Make your business more profitable.

13) Make your business successful.

14) Achieve Business Goals.

Let me tell you a real-life story about my client Kris Welch [name changed], I met him at a business conference. He was operating a

Home improvement business.

He started his business thinking that he will be independent and will be free from the 9 to 5 job. All was good in the beginning, he got clients through his friends and family. But after a few months, as the referrals died and he started facing the practical difficulties of running a business, things came crippling down.

He started thinking about whether he has done the right thing by quitting his job and starting his own business. This was his first year of business, his business was one of the five businesses that were on the brink of failing.

This was when he asked for my help. When I analyzed his Business, there were no operating systems in place, cash flow management was poor, there was no organizational structure, he didn't have any goal, no road map, no business plan, and no marketing plan and he didn't have any brand in the local market.

After I helped him completely restructure his business, now he is generating more than $1 million in revenue from a single location and is planning to expand to other cities as quickly as possible.

The issues because of which Kris was failing in his business are the most common problems that most businesses have. These are the typical reasons why most businesses fail.

Trust me I know, after failing 2 businesses, I was determined to learn the proper ways and the secrets of succeeding in business. I put in a lot of effort, read a lot of books, and collected wisdom from different persons and sources. Finally, I was able to figure out how to achieve success in any business.

I have mentioned some of the wisdom that I have learned over the years here in this, Business Unlocked book.

If you want to be successful in your business then you need to read this book. Remember, only reading is not enough. 20% is reading and learning, rest 80% is implementation.

Let's begin.

PART 1 – RESEARCH

CHAPTER 1 - FIND YOUR WHY

If you are planning to start a business. The first thing you should do is ask yourself, why do you want to start this particular business? Or if you have already started one, why are you doing it? What's your motivation and the main reason behind it, why do you choose this particular business out of thousands of businesses out there in the world?

Find out what your WHY is. Whether it is to retire with millions of dollars in your bank, or you want to travel the globe, or you want to change the world in some way. Your WHY can be one of the few mentioned here or can be as unique as you. Your WHY should be the one that you connect deeply with.

The deeper your WHY will be, the more successful you will be in your business. Your success depends on whether your WHY is deep enough so that it drives enough motivation for you to achieve your goals.

Find Your WHY: The Secret to Motivating Yourself and Others in Business

If you were to ask the majority of successful business leaders about what makes them tick, almost all would answer with some version of the same thing: their WHY. WHY do they get out of bed in the morning? WHY do they put up with all the stress and sacrifices that come with running their own company? It's because they have a burning belief — their WHY — that drives everything they do. It's the one thing that gives them purpose in life and makes them unafraid of failure or rejection.

On the other hand, one of the common things with people that are not successful is, they don't have a passion for what they are doing or a reason for being in their business. They don't have a driving force behind their activities. They're just drifting through life, looking for the next big thing.

In business, it's easy to get caught up in the day-to-day grind. While keeping tabs on inventory and sales, meeting quarterly objectives, and managing all of your employees can help you run an effective company ... but it doesn't help you stand out from the crowd. If you want to make a lasting impact with your company, think about why you got into the business in the first place.

At some point in your business, you may feel like you've hit a wall —perhaps even wondering if this is as good as it gets. It's at these times that we must dig deep to find our WHY—that one phrase that sums up why we do what we do.

Once you discover your WHY, you can better understand what drives you to achieve the best version of YOU. You should keep this WHY in your mind while doing everything that you do to give your absolute best in everything that you do.

Remember a WHY is the reason you get up in the morning. It's your reason for being - your core belief that drives everything you do.

Everyone has a WHY, even if they don't realize it. Finding it, however, can help you discover the motivation and inspiration to push through the tough times when business gets slow, cash flow gets tight and employees are getting anxious.

What's the difference between a person who has a WHY and a person who just keeps on with the daily grind of business without knowing the reason why he is doing all that hard work? The WHY gives a person a sense of purpose and inspires them to keep moving forward. On the other hand, the person who doesn't have a WHY is always stressed and tired of the business activities, because they don't have a reason to grind hard day after day. It's not that they're not hard-working or any less talented, it's simply that they lack motivation because they don't know their purpose of being in the business in the first place.

How to find your WHY

When you're looking for your Why, it's important to have the right mindset. You have to be open to discovering new things about yourself and your life. The process is about finding your passion and inspiration. It's about inspiring others around you as well.

These are some key points for finding your WHY:

Start with the end in mind: Sit down and ask yourself, what you want your life to stand for? What do you want to be remembered for? What is the one message you want to spread to the world?

Identify your core values: What are your core values? Think about it, for example, the best teachers you had growing up, What made them such effective teachers? What made them stand out? What were they passionate about? What was their WHY? The best teachers have a way of getting their students excited and engaged in the subject. They don't just deliver information, they find a way to inspire you.

Uncover your strengths: What are you good at? What are your strengths? What are the things you enjoy doing? This is a great way to get a glimpse of your WHY. Why do you gravitate toward certain tasks, subjects, or activities?

Recognize your core fears: What are you afraid of? What has stopped you from achieving your goals and dreams in the past? What stands in the way of you achieving your life goals?

Be open: Be willing to let go of your preconceived notions about who you are and what you're capable of.

Be patient: For most finding their WHY isn't quick and easy. It's a process that takes time.

Be Honest: It requires you to be honest with yourself and get out of your own way. Your WHY doesn't need to be ideally perfect. You have to stop letting your fears hold you back from being all that you can be.

Take help from your life experiences: When you get stuck, think about the highlights of your life so far. What have been the most amazing or significant moments in your life? How did those experiences make you feel? What did you learn from those experiences?

Get feedback: As you make progress on your journey of self-discovery, it's important to get feedback. Have one-on-one conversations with trusted friends, family members, and mentors. Ask for their help so that you can listen to their version of your personality. This might help you realize things about yourself that you overlooked.

Making everyone know your WHY is important for business growth

While finding your WHY is important, so is making it known to others. If you want to make an impact with your company, you need to get your WHY out into the public sphere. You need to start connecting with people on a deeper level — finding ways to inspire them and get them excited to buy your product or service.

When you make your WHY known, you make it easier for others to connect with you, trust you and do business with you. People want to buy from people who they believe in. They want to do business with people who have something to stand for. They want to buy from people who are genuine, authentic, and have something unique to offer.

The WHY is behind everything you do. It's the driving force behind your activities, the reason why you get out of bed in the morning, the reason why you do what you do, and the reason why other people should do business with you. It's the thing that makes you unique, and the thing that inspires others to follow you. It's the thing that keeps you going when things get tough, and the thing that gives you strength to fight failure.

CHAPTER 2 - PROBLEM SOLVING ANALYSIS

The reason my first business failed was that my only focus was how to earn money quickly, I did not focus on the problems my target customers were facing. After this failure, I understood that one can be in business for a long time only when one solves the problem of one's customers, which makes these customers come back again.

For solving the problem of your customers first you need to know and understand what problems your target customers have. If you do not know what problems your customers have, then how you will provide a solution to them?

Remember your product or service needs to solve at least one problem of your target customers, this is one of the keys to a long-lasting profitable business. If you can solve more than one problem, you have got yourself a goldmine there.

Problem solving analysis is an approach for analyzing customer problems so that these problems can be effectively resolved. It is a problem solving technique used to identify customer issues and transform them into opportunities for your business.

As a business owner, it's important to be able to identify and solve customer problems with your product or service. By doing so, you can ensure customer satisfaction and loyalty, which will in turn lead to repeat business and referrals.

Before you begin solving customer problems with your product or service, it is important to understand why and how frequently customers are having issues. This will not only help you understand how to solve the problems but also identify the demand for your new product or service.

Why is problem solving analysis important?

Problem solving analysis is important for a number of reasons. It allows you to understand what problems your customers are facing, which can help you in creating new products, including new features, to solve customer issues. If you have existing products on the market by doing problem solving analysis you can find and fill any gaps in your product line.

The better you understand the problems your customers are encountering, the more likely you are to be able to develop effective solutions for those problems. Using problem solving analysis can help you to create solutions that are not only effective but also improve your customer's satisfaction with your products and overall experience with your company.

Solving customer problems has many benefits for both businesses and customers. By providing solutions to customers' problems, businesses can build trust and loyalty, increase sales, and improve their reputation. Customers also benefit from having their problems solved, as they can find products or services that better meet their needs and improve their overall experience with a business.

Some of the benefits include:
- Understand the problem from the customer's perspective
- Identify the root cause of the problem
- Develop potential solutions to the problem
- Evaluate the effectiveness of each potential solution
- Choose the most effective solution to implement
- Reduced customer dissatisfaction and complaints
- Improved customer service and support
- Increased customer loyalty
- Increased sales and business efficiency
- Improved product quality
- Increased customer satisfaction
- Improved product functionality
- Increased market demand for your product or service
- Improved product/company image

Determine which problem to solve first

When you are conducting problem solving analysis, you may identify several issues that your customers are experiencing. However, before you start to solve these problems, it's important to determine which problems to solve first. This can be done by evaluating the problem's frequency and severity.

Frequency: The more often customers are experiencing problems, the higher priority the problem should be.

Severity: The higher the impact a problem has on the customer, the more important it is to solve the problem.

The type of problem you decide to solve will determine the solution that you select.

Identify the cause of the problem

Once you've identified potential customer problems, it's important to analyze them to understand the root cause of the issue. This will help you determine how to best solve the problem.

Once you've found the root cause of the problem, you can start generating potential solutions. Be sure to involve your team in this process so that you can get different perspectives on how to best solve the problem.

You need to offer a solution that solves that problem. Your solution could be a new product or service, or it could be an existing product or service that you modify to better meet the needs of your customers. Either way, your goal is to provide a solution that meets the customer's needs and addresses their pain points.

Select the right solution

The next step in problem solving analysis is to select the right solution. There are a few factors to consider when selecting the right solution, such as:

Cost: How much will it cost to implement the solution?

Time: How long will it take to implement the solution?

Risk: What is the risk associated with implementing the solution?

Resources: What resources will be needed to implement the solution?

Value: How much will the solution add to your product?

Your product or service should be designed with the customer's problem in mind. Every aspect of your offering should be focused on solving the customer's problem in the most effective way possible. When customers see how your product or service solves their problem, they will be more likely to use it and recommend it to others.

Once you have determined the solution, you can start developing a finalized solution. This means creating a plan for how you will implement the solution, including any steps or procedures necessary to bring the solution to life.

When it comes to problem solving, it's important to first understand what the problem is and why it matters. Once you've identified the problem, you can then offer a solution that solves it. Not only will this improve customer satisfaction, but it will also benefit your business in the long run. Remember analyzing and solving customer problems is important and gives you a competitive edge over your competitors and helps you get your rightful place in the market.

CHAPTER 3 - DEMAND ANALYSIS

Demand analysis is the process of evaluating how much demand a product or service has, whether it's enough to continue selling the current product or introduce a new one, and if there are any red flags, this indicates the product might not be worth selling or continuing to sell.

Understanding when and why you should conduct a demand analysis will help you achieve business success.
Demand analysis is the process of evaluating how many units of a product or a company expects to sell over an extended period. This would include an analysis of the product's price, the target audience, and other relevant factors to come up with a projected or estimated sales volume for a specified period.

Remember, demand analysis can be conducted at any time, whether you're planning to introduce a new product or service to the market or you wish to determine the future demand for your current product or service.

When to Conduct a Demand Analysis

Conducting a demand analysis is a must before launching your product or service. It should also be conducted in the following circumstances:

When you are contemplating to:
Improve an existing product or service or
Add a new feature to an existing product or service.

After you have conducted the analysis, you will be in a better position to determine whether it is in your best interest to pursue the opportunity.

If it is, you will have a good idea of how much effort and resources it will take to get your product or service ready for launch. You will also know how much investment would be needed initially to get your business up and running.

Why is a Demand Analysis Important?

Demand analysis is important for several reasons. It allows you to estimate the demand for a product or service before you actually go to the market with it.

If a product doesn't have high demand, there's no point in wasting time and money on developing a strategy that has no potential to succeed. On the other hand, a product with high demand will likely be a profitable investment for your business. The analysis can help you determine whether the product will be worth your time and money to proceed.

It also allows you to estimate the profit potential of your product or service. It allows you to estimate the price that customers are willing to pay for your product or service. You can determine whether or not the market is large enough for your proposed product or service.

If you are a manufacturer you will order raw materials based on your demand analysis, or if you are a trader you will order finished products based on it.

Product Demand Analysis helps businesses:

1. To know whether the proposed product would be profitable even before actually spending anything on its production.

2. To forecast sales. Sales forecasts are important for every business. This helps businesses to be better prepared for achieving the highest possible sales.

3. To help perform financial planning better by estimating the requirement of money and other resources needed for product development and production.

4. To make better decisions about the allocation of money and other resources.

5. To identify new markets for its products and to develop new products that are more accessible to consumers.

6. To improve its sales and marketing efforts and to attract new customers.

7. To better understand customers' needs and preferences. This enables businesses to develop products that are more popular and profitable.

8. To determine the pricing policy. It helps businesses to determine the price of the product or service that will be most profitable.

9. To customize the production policy. The more demand for the product is projected, the higher quantity of the product will be produced.

How to Perform a Demand Analysis

There isn't a singular formula or method for conducting a demand analysis. However, there are a few factors you should consider when conducting your analysis. A demand analysis will likely include information about the product's target audience, the product's price, and the product's sales cycle.

There are no set rules for conducting a demand analysis. It's important that you understand the factors that will affect the analysis and use them to create an analysis that's best for your business.

If you want to sell a physical product, whether online or offline, one quick tip for you. Go and check Amazon's best-selling products in your niche and you will exactly find what are the current products that are selling well.

One of the best ways to determine the demand for your product is to go to https://trends.google.com/trends/ and type your niche or product name.

Here you can select the state or country, the past number of months, your category, and whether you want to search through the web search or Google Shopping. If you have a physical product, I recommend checking both the web search data and Google Shopping data.

For success, you need to have a good demand for your product. I recommend that your product should have at least 50 points in interest over time in your niche.

While conducting demand analysis you also have to note down whether your category comes in essential or not and what are its uses. Suppose it's a food product that is consumed every day so it will be essential and these products' demand is much higher as compared to non-essential products.

Also, you have to categorize whether your product satisfies, customer needs or it satisfies their leisure. Although leisure products have less demand, however, the profit margin is usually higher than the products that satisfy the needs of the customers. Keep all these things in mind while performing demand analysis. All this will help you find what is the profit potential of your product.

Remember, demand analysis is essential. It is one of the initial building blocks for your new product or service. It is one of the first steps to success.

CHAPTER 4 - COMPETITION RESEARCH

Competition research is a strategic process that enables you to learn more about your competitors and their strategies. This will help you understand what threats they pose, how to counter them, and also which opportunities you can capitalize on as an advantage for your business.

Competition research is not just about learning more about your competitors; it's about focusing on the right things so that your strategy has an impact on the market rather than just being another company trying to survive.
The importance of competition research cannot be stressed enough in today's business landscape.

Customers now have more options than ever before when it comes to where they spend their money. Any company looking to stay ahead of the curve needs a solid understanding of its competitors.

Competitive analysis can act as valuable insight into your industry and helps you determine the potential threats or opportunities that lie ahead.

It is essential to understand the strengths and weaknesses of your business in order to identify areas for growth and remain focused on what you're good at.

To do this, you need a competition research strategy. This will help you to scope out your chosen market and find the information you need to make informed strategic decisions. A well-thought-out plan will save you time and effort as well as ensure that all of your bases are covered.

Competition is not essentially bad, it can be a good thing. Though it means that there are other businesses out there trying to offer something similar, it also means there's a market for your product or service. But how do you know if your business has the potential to thrive in that particular market? How do you know if your business can compete effectively? Competition research is the answer.

Competition research is a source of invaluable insight into your competitors' strategies and the market at large.

What is a Competition Research?

Competition research is a thorough investigation into your competitors, their products and services, their marketing plans, as well as their strengths and weaknesses.

It is an essential process that will help you learn more about the market and identify potential threats and opportunities that could impact your business. It will also give you an idea of the industry as a whole and help you to understand where your business sits within that framework.

Competition research will help you to identify who your

competitors are, where they are in the market, and how they are positioning themselves compared to you. It will also provide you with valuable insights that will help you to improve your business.

The purpose of competition research is to know your competitors better than they know themselves. To thoroughly understand your competitors will require you to know them better than they know themselves. You need to know your competitors as if you were in their shoes.

You don't need to know everything about your competitors. You just need to know the information that will be helpful to your strategy. You don't need to know the names of every employee at your competitor's company. But, you do need to know their weaknesses and how you can use that information against them.

Why is Competition Research Important?

The main benefit of competition research is to know what are their strengths and weaknesses. You cannot succeed if you don't know what your competitors are doing. So it is very important to note down every aspect of competitors, including their marketing and sales tactics.

Understanding your competition will help you to make strategic decisions that will positively impact your business. Competition research will help you to identify where your competitors are strongest, and where you can find opportunities to grow your business. It will help you to capture the market share for your new product or service.

Essentially, it will allow you to better understand your market and what you are up against. This will also allow you to make more informed decisions that can help you to stay ahead of the curve and make your business stronger.

Competition research will help you to see where your competitors are investing, what they're promoting, and what they are doing to get their name out there. How many followers do they have on different social media such as Twitter, Facebook, Pinterest, etc. Are they applying any other marketing tactics like webinars or podcasts?

What are the advertising campaigns they are running, whether they are online or offline, and what type of content they are publishing on their blog?

You can find how your competitors are presenting their brand in front of the customers. You can identify their gaps in marketing and hiring processes. And analyze your gaps in marketing processes.

Competition research can also help you to identify important trends in the market and allow you to plan accordingly.

You can analyze what are the different services or products they are offering to the customers. You can also analyze who are they targeting.

If they have a physical product, whether they are selling on Amazon or Walmart or different stores, what are the number of SKUs they have, and what are the price points they are offering.

All this will help you identify where they are falling short and where you can step in with a better solution.

Identify Your Competitors

When conducting your competition research, it's important to find the right information so you can make the most of your research.

The first step in this process will be to identify the competitors that are most relevant to your industry. This may include companies that produce similar products, or have the same services as you. Also, note down how many competitors you have in your market.

Though this can be somewhat tricky, especially if you're in an industry with a lot of smaller players. It can be helpful to think about your competitors in terms of brand, product, and service. This will allow you to look at your competitors in a broader sense, as opposed to narrowly defining them.

If you're having trouble identifying your competitors, try brainstorming. Jot down a few names that come to mind and list out their positive and negative aspects. Once you've identified your competitors, you should take some time to do further research.

Ideally, you want to have an idea of their general size, who they cater to, their strengths, and their weaknesses. You can do this by reading their blog posts, visiting their website, and going through their social media posts. This will help you to get a better understanding of your competition and allow you to compare them to your own business.

Identify Your Differentiators

Once you know who your competitors are, you should also take the time to identify your differentiators. These are the strengths that set your business apart from the competition.

Identifying your differentiators will allow you to compare your business to your competitors more effectively and help you to understand where you excel or can excel.

This can be helpful when you're creating a marketing strategy or developing new products and services. You may want to use a checklist to help you determine your differentiators.

You can use the same list to look at your competitors' strengths as well. This will allow you to dive deeper into each of these areas and help you to identify opportunities for improvement.

How to Perform Effective Competition Research?

Now that you understand the basics of conducting a competition analysis, you can begin to put your research plan into action. There are a few different ways that you can go about collecting your data. You could use a competitive intelligence tool, you could use Google (or another search engine) to collect your data, you could use social media monitoring tools to collect your data, or you can talk to industry experts.

- Competitive Intelligence Tools: Using a competitive intelligence tool is a great way to go about conducting your competition research. Some of the tools you can use are Similarweb, Semrush, G2 Crowd, etc. These tools provide you with insights into your competitors.

They will also allow you to look at their marketing strategies and provide you with information on their social media presence. These tools can be helpful if you want to gain an in-depth understanding of your competition.

- Google (or another search engine): If you decide to go this route, make sure that you're using the right keywords. It's a good idea to use a tool like Google Trends to see which keywords are popular and how your competitors are using them. This will help you to identify general keyword trends and will provide you with information on how competitors are using keywords.

It will also allow you to look at what terms people are searching for and what information they're trying to find. This can be helpful if you just want a general overview of your competitors.

- Social Media Monitoring Tools: These tools are helpful if you want to stay on top of the latest trends in your industry. You can use these tools to monitor your competitors' social media channels and keep track of their marketing campaigns. Some of the social media monitoring tools are Hootsuite, Nexalogy, Mentionlytics, etc.

They will also allow you to look at your competitors' follower counts and allow you to see what people are saying about them. This can be helpful if you want to keep an eye on your competition but don't have time to comb through everything they put out there.

- Talk to the Industry Experts - Another good way to find information about your competitors is to talk to people who are experts in your industry. These individuals are often great sources of information about different businesses in your industry, as well as the strategies they are employing.

Competition research takes time. It can't be done in a day, nor should it be. You want to take the time to do it right so that your strategy is as effective as it can be.

Now that you've conducted your competition analysis, you need to determine what to do with your findings. You can use the information that you've collected to make strategic decisions that can help you to improve your business.

You can also use it to create a marketing strategy that allows you to stand out from the crowd. This will help you to connect with your target audience and provide them with a solution to their problems.

After analyzing the competition, you can improve your product or services. You can better create your unique selling proposition.

CHAPTER 5 -
UNIQUE SELLING
PROPOSITION (USP)

A Unique Selling Proposition or USP is your main "selling point." It's something that makes your product stand out from its competitors.

We live in a very competitive marketplace, with new businesses launching every day. To stand out from the crowd and drive more traffic to your store you need a strong brand identity and a distinct selling proposition for your target audience.

In today's world, it's become more important than ever for you to have a clear and concise way to explain to the customers why they should choose your product over others.

A good USP does not need to be complicated; the simpler it is the more effective it will be.

Remember your Unique Selling Proposition needs to be concise, memorable, and logical.

If you want to succeed, you need to have a USP for your product or service. Without it, the customer won't buy your product. Instead, they will go to your competitor who is already a well-established brand.

The idea behind a USP is that no one else is offering exactly what you are. This is called creating a "unique" value proposition because it's something that nobody else can copy.

That's not to say, that you should have only one positive feature in your product or service. You should try to incorporate as many features as possible!

A USP is something that makes people see your business, product, or service as being better than any other comparable alternative in the market. Think of it as a single-sentence statement that tells potential customers, why they should buy from you rather than someone else.

There are many reasons why every business should have a USP, let's see a few here.

It allows you to set yourself apart from the competition. If all of your competitors are providing the same products and services as you are, you need a USP that makes you unique and shows potential customers why they should choose to do business with you.

Your USP can help you attract attention and get noticed in a very noisy marketplace.

Your USP is also important for branding. Your brand is the image that people associate with your company. Your brand is essentially the mental image that customers have of your company.

Your brand and your USP go hand in hand. If you don't have a strong USP or one that's poorly developed, your brand won't be as effective.

How to Develop a Unique Selling Proposition

Now as you know the importance of a USP. Let's look at how you can develop one for your product or service.

When it comes to developing a USP, there are a few different ways that you can go with it.

You can look at the competition and see what they're doing. What are their advertisements like? What promises or slogans are they using? What are their products' biggest advantages? What are customers saying about their products? Take note of what makes your competitors' products unique and how they're being marketed to customers.

Another way to develop your USP is to look at your product. What makes your product unique? What are its biggest advantages? What makes it better than the competition?

Another tactic is to look at the customer and their needs. What problems do customers have that your product can solve? What are the customers' biggest pain points? What do customers want or need that your product can provide for them?

Once you've brainstormed a few ideas for your USP, test them out. Test out different slogans or taglines, or write out different promises that your product or service could make. See which ones resonate with your target audience and which ones don't.

It is important that your USP should be,

Clear and Concise

It's important to not only tell the customer what your product is, but also how it works. It's a good idea to explain the benefits of your product. A strong USP will help you sell your product to more people and drive more traffic to your store. If you can not explain clearly, it means you don't have a strong USP.

If you want to stand out from other companies who are already established in their market segment, make sure that your USP is clear and concise so that customers can easily understand what exactly this product does or how it works.

It's important to be as specific as possible when describing your product or service because it will help customers understand exactly what they are buying at once.

The more complex the selling point is, the harder it will be for customers to understand, what exactly they are buying because they have no context for understanding what exactly this product does or how it works.

If you want to stand out from other companies, who are already established in their market segment, make sure that your USP is clear and concise so that customers can easily understand what exactly this product does or how it works.

Memorable

The first thing that customers will notice about your product or service is how it looks, smells, or feels. That's why it's so important that you make sure that your USP is memorable and easy to remember. Your USP should be something that customers can easily relate to, and they will remember it for a long time. The more unique the selling point is, there is better chance of generating repeated sales.

Logical and simple

It's important to keep things simple when describing your product or service; everything must be explained in one sentence so that customers can understand at once what exactly they are buying.

There are a few things that make a good USP. Your USP should be memorable, it should be relevant to your customers' needs and wants. It should also be something that is easily understandable and relatable.

When you're testing out different slogans or promises for your product, ask yourself if your USP is something that customers would remember.

Is it something that they could tell their friends about? Is it relatable to the problems your customers are facing? Consider how your USP could be interpreted by your customers.

Your USP can help you to stand out from the crowd and drive more traffic to your store. It can also help you to brand yourself as an industry leader and build a loyal customer base. Create something memorable that your customers can easily relate to and remember, and you'll be well on your way to success.

CHAPTER 6 –
TESTING YOUR IDEA
OR PRODUCT

Let me start this chapter with a real-life example. One of my clients who is in the dog care niche, manufactures dog toys, he designed a new unique toy and he thought it would sell pretty well, he manufactured more than 30000 pcs, but then when he tried to sell it, less than 100 pcs sold, he faced the loss of more than $60000, now if you are a small business owner you know the value of $60000.

Testing helps you succeed. Those who are successful in gold mining don't just start digging the land to find gold. Instead, they dig small holes and test that sample for the weight of gold, if that sample contains enough gold then they bring all the equipment and start digging to extract gold, with this technique they save a lot of time, money, and energy.

As a business owner, you're likely to have some great ideas for new products or services that you can bring to market. However, testing them first is always recommended. Whether it's a new product, process, or service; testing an idea is essential in ensuring its success before spending too much time and money on it.

I have seen a lot of businesses make the mistake of not testing their product, they think that their product will be a huge success in the market and they manufacture in bulk, but when they try to sell their product it does not sell and they blame the economy, customers, etc.
Your initial idea might seem great at first but after some testing and critical thinking, it might not be as solid as you first thought.

Many business owners believe in their idea or product and are sure it's going to change the world. So they manufacture in bulk or order in bulk, hoping they'll sell it with a high-profit margin. But that doesn't happen often. And when it doesn't, most of us are left with this big question mark in our heads: Why? That feeling of disappointment generally means: They didn't test their idea or product well enough.

As an aspiring entrepreneur and not just another dreamer, it is important to test your idea before implementing it big time.

You're probably convinced that your product is the best idea ever, but do you know for certain? It's important to test your product or idea as early as possible. That's because you're going to get insights on things like - Is there a demand for this product? Can people understand the value of it? Will they actually purchase it? These are all important questions that you need to answer before investing any time, effort, or money in your product.

If your idea is for a new product or service, testing it will help you find out if your product or service actually solves a problem for people, and if there's any interest in it.

Before putting too much time, money, and effort into any project, it's important to test it first to make sure it's actually worth all that effort. Otherwise, you could be throwing a lot of time and money away on something that no one wants. It's important to keep in mind that not every idea is a winner and that yours might not be an exception.

I am writing all this not to discourage you from your ideas. My intention is to make you realize the power of testing so that you know which of your great ideas are actually worth your time, money, and effort. Which are the ones that will give you success as a business owner.

How to Test Your Product or Service Before Launching It

Step 1 - Define Your Audience Before Developing Or Launching A Product

Once you've got some basic information on your product and its potential customers, it's time to take it a step further and define your customers. Who will be using your product or service? - Why will they be using it? - How will they use it? How do they behave? What do they like? What do they dislike? How do they spend their time? What are their frustrations? You can do this by simply creating a survey or questionnaire and asking your potential customers a few questions.

A product or service might seem like a good idea on paper; however, it might not work out in real life because you're not addressing the needs of your customers. You can learn a lot about your potential customers by simply asking them some questions. It's a simple process that can make or break your product or service before you even launch it. You should have already done this in the product demand analysis step.

Step 2 - Beta Test and Run an A/B Product or Service Testing Experiment

Manufacture a small batch of your product with different variations and test them on a small group of people to see if they like it. You can launch a beta version of your product or service and sell those to customers. If you are a service provider then you need to get at least 5 customers.

An A/B testing experiment is a great way to test your product or service before it's even developed. This is essentially where you create two different versions of your product or service and let your potential customers choose which one they like more.

You can do this by creating two different value propositions for your product or service. Now you just need to get those in front of your customers and see which one they respond to more. A/B testing can be very helpful if one of your product ideas is around the packaging or design of the product. It's important to keep in mind that you can't test too many things at once with an A/B testing experiment.

Step 3 - Gather User Feedback

Before you launch your product or service, always make sure you gather feedback from your customers. This way, you'll know if you're addressing the needs of your customers with your product or service.

Feedback will help you improve your product or service and you will exactly know what are the flaws in your product. It's also important that you don't release any final version of your product or service until you have received enough feedback from real customers.

You can get feedback in a few different ways: - Create a survey or questionnaire for your customers or Host an online forum or discussion where you invite your customers to participate. It's important to keep in mind that whatever you're doing, you want your customers' feedback to be honest and constructive.

Ideas can come and go, but the execution is what matters. You might have the best idea in the world, but if you never take action and follow through on it, it will never become a reality. But what you need to keep in mind is that testing is an important step before you bring your ideas into reality by investing time and money into them.

CHAPTER 7 -
IRRESISTIBLE OFFER

Creating an irresistible offer is a great way to get customers to buy. You know what they say, you can put anything on a shelf, but that doesn't mean they will necessarily buy it. People will only purchase if something compels them to do so.

Intentionally designing your products and services with an irresistible offer in mind can help you sell more of your products faster by creating a situation in which customers want to buy from you.

However, putting up some random sale won't work for long-term brand building and growth as a business owner. For this reason, coming up with ways to trigger people into buying your goods is essential for establishing a steady stream of sales that continues over time as well as expanding your customer base and attracting new customers who will continue making purchases from you again in the future.

An irresistible offer is something that compels people to make a purchase. This might be something like an offer for free shipping or a limited-time discount.

However, an irresistible offer can be more than that. It can be a guarantee that the product will solve an important problem for the customer. In short, creating an irresistible offer is about meeting customer needs and wants, and giving them a reason to buy from you that they can't get anywhere else.

It's important to note that a good offer is something that customers can't refuse. It's something they can't say no to. If you can create an irresistible offer, you are essentially putting a product or service in front of your customers that solve their problems. So never underestimate the power of a good offer.

The more an offer is attractive, the more likely that it will be accepted. You should always aim to keep your customers happy and satisfied with your product or service.

Creating an Irresistible Offer

There is no one-size-fits-all formula for creating an irresistible offer. However, there are a few key elements that can help you get started when creating your irresistible offer.

First, think about the benefits of your product or service. What does it do for the customer? What are the problems it solves for them? Once you have a clear idea of the benefits of your products or services, try to find ways to make those benefits even more irresistible to your customers by adding something extra for your customers.

Try to think of creative ways to emphasize the benefits of your products or services. Show these benefits in your product packaging.

Next, think about what your customers want. If you are selling a product, think about how and where your target customers would use it. If you are selling a service, think about how it helps the customer. Try to find ways to make your product or service even more consistent in meeting the needs of your customers.

An example of an irresistible offer is selling a great product with 'no questions asked' money-back guarantee, you are making an offer that is very attractive to customers. If you are a service-based business you can work on a performance basis this will make an attractive offer for your clients.

You can think about what offer you can give to your customers to give them something extra over a great-performing product to make sure they buy your product and come back to buy more in the future.

Even if you have a few great ideas for creating an irresistible offer, you don't want to commit to a single campaign and hope for the best. Rather, you want to test and track the effectiveness of each campaign so you know which is the most effective. You want to try a few campaigns at the same time to see which creates the most impact and results. For example, you can also offer an incentive like a limited-time discount or a free shipping offer.

Creating an irresistible offer is an essential part of growing your business. It is a great way to drive customers to make a purchase. However, you need to make sure that you are creating an offer that will appeal to customers. The offer should solve a problem and should make the customer feel special. Customers should feel like they can't refuse your offer.

PART 2 – GOALS AND PLANNING

CHAPTER 8 - SMART BUSINESS GOALS

Setting and achieving business goals is essential to the success of any company.

Your business goals are the specific objectives that you want to achieve with your business. They can be short-term goals, such as increasing sales by 10% in the next quarter, or long-term goals, such as becoming the market leader in your industry.

Every company has different objectives, and it's important to set measurable goals to stay on track. A SMART goal is a goal that is specific, measurable, achievable, relevant and time-bound.

Specific goals: Specific enough that you can track your progress towards them.

Measurable goals: It should be easy to measure progress towards the goal.

Achievable goals: They should be realistic and achievable, within the given timeframe.

Relevant goals: They should be relevant to your overall objectives and values.

Time-bound goals: Goals should have a deadline or a time frame by which they must be reached.

It is important to set SMART goals because they allow you to set a path toward your business success. This is because they give you a clear idea of what you need to achieve and by when. This means that you will have a better idea of where your business needs to go and by what time in the future it will reach there.

You can use the SMART method to create better goals for your company. Whether you're just starting out or you've been in business for some time, setting goals is important. If you have set your goals, you can measure your success easily. If you need to grow your business, setting goals will keep you on track.

Setting SMART goals can be a very helpful way to achieve your desired outcomes.

How to Set SMART Goals for Your Company

Achieving success with your business requires careful planning and execution. By following these guidelines, you'll be well on your way to achieving your business goals and ensuring a bright future for your company.

First, choose which goal is most important: At the outset, you'll need to decide which business goal is most important to you. This means that you will need to choose between different goals and figure out which is the most important one.

Write down your goal: Once you've chosen a goal, you'll need to write it down. You can write it down on paper, or you can type it into a document on your computer.

Break down your goal into smaller pieces: Once you've written your goal down, it's time to break it down. You don't want your goal to stay at the general level – you need to get more specific.

Make sure your goal is SMART: Once you've got your goal broken down as much as possible, make sure that it meets the SMART criteria.

Set a deadline for your goal: Once you've broken down your goal and made it SMART, it's time to set a deadline. Don't let your goal remain a general idea – make sure you set a date by which you want to achieve it.

For executing your goal it is essential that you set your yearly business goals or vision. From here you will divide this goal into the smaller time frame.

Like based on a one-year goal you will set your quarterly targets. After that based on quarterly targets decide your monthly goals and based on monthly decide your weekly target.

It is vital that you analyze your goals periodically like whether you were able to achieve the goal that you had set for the last month or not, and if not what were its reasons and how you can improve it, this same applies to quarterly and yearly targets.

It is ideal to set a 10 min daily meeting every morning to decide your daily work target to achieve your weekly goals.

There are several benefits of setting SMART goals.

Focus: Firstly, they allow you to be more focused. If you have a specific goal in mind, you are less likely to be distracted by other things. Setting goals can be a very beneficial activity in business. Goals can help you focus your efforts, identify areas where you need to improve and provide a measure of accomplishment. It gives you a sense of direction and purpose for your business. Additionally, setting goals can help you be on the track during challenging times.

Time Efficient: It allows you to be more efficient with your time. Once you have a goal in mind, you will know how to spend your time in the best way possible.

Measurement: It makes it easier to measure your success. If you have a specific goal in mind, you will be able to look back and see how successful you were.

Communication: It also makes it easier to communicate with others. If your team members understand your goals, they will be able to work better together.

Motivation: It is also a form of motivation. If you are working towards a goal, you will be motivated to achieve it.

If you're working towards business goals with a team of people, it's important that everyone is on the same page and working towards the same objectives. To hold yourself accountable, make sure that your team members are aware of the goals they need to accomplish and check in with them regularly about their progress.

You can also use tools like task management software or project management software to help track everyone's progress and ensure that everyone is meeting their deadlines.

If you want your business to be successful, you need to set clear and achievable goals. A well-thought-out business plan is essential for success, and setting goals is an important part of the process. Make sure your goals are specific, measurable, attainable, relevant, and time-bound. Write them down and create a plan to achieve them.

These goals will help you track your progress, provide a blueprint for success, and keep you motivated. Make sure your goals are

SMART, and you'll be in a great position to achieve your business goals. Hold yourself and your team accountable to your goals, and don't forget to review and adjust them as needed.

CHAPTER 9 - BUSINESS PLAN

On average 70% of entrepreneurs launch their business without a business plan.

As per Benjamin Franklin - "If You Fail to Plan, You Are Planning to Fail", this means that it will be very difficult to achieve success if you do not have a plan. With a proper plan, you will exactly know where you want to go and how you will reach there.

From Business to Government, everyone needs a plan to achieve goals. If you see the most successful people, they have proper plans for their life.

Whether you are thinking of starting a business? Or maybe you want to take your business to the next level. Either way, you'll need a business plan.

A business plan is your roadmap to success. It is a document that encompasses all areas of your business and works as a strategic plan and a practical tool.

A business plan is a document that outlines your company's objectives and strategies for achieving those objectives. A business plan can be tailored to the needs of an organization. It can be extensive, covering every aspect of an operation, or it can be brief and general, outlining the key components of a company.

A business plan is both a strategic and a practical document. It helps you think strategically about the future of your company while acting as a road map to help you make decisions regarding day-to-day operations. Most business plans include information about the target market, competitors, and industry trends; financial projections; marketing plans; and operational procedures.

Investors are more likely to fund businesses with well-written, detailed business plans. A well-written business plan will not only help you secure financing from investors but also help you remain focused as an entrepreneur during challenging times.

A business plan can help almost any type of company succeed. It can be especially useful for new businesses that have little operating history and cannot rely on personal reputation as their main selling point. Even established companies can benefit from having a detailed strategy that can be updated regularly as the company changes and grows.

Essentially, it's a road map for your business. Creating a business plan will force you to think critically about what you want to achieve with your business and how you're going to get there.

Before writing your Business Plan consider the following points:

What does your business do?

Your business plan should start with a clear definition of what your business does. This might seem like a simple task, but it's important to be as specific as possible in order to give potential investors and partners a good sense of what you're all about.

For example, if you're starting a new restaurant, you might define your business as follows:

"XYZ Restaurant will be a full-service eatery serving traditional American cuisine. We will focus on providing fresh, made-from-scratch dishes at affordable prices. Our target market will be families and young professionals living in the XYZ area."

This gives readers a good overview of what your business does, who it will serve, and what kind of experience they can expect.

Who is your target market

To make your business successful, you need to have a clear understanding of who your target market is. This means identifying the specific group of people who are most likely to use your products or services.

For example, if you're starting a new fitness studio, your target market might be defined as follows:

"Our target market will be health-conscious individuals living in the XYZ area who are looking for an alternative to traditional gyms."

Once you've identified your target market, you can then tailor your marketing efforts (including your advertising, branding, and messaging) to appeal directly to them.

Understand the market trends

When you're creating a business plan, it's important to understand the market trends for your industry. This will help you determine your place in the market, what needs exist that you can fill, and how to reach your target audience. You can find this information through online research, talking to experts in your field, or attending industry events.

Know your competition

A key part of any business plan is understanding who your competition is and what they're doing well—or not so well. This research will help you determine how to position your own business to be successful. To learn about your competition, start by searching online, reading trade publications, or talking to people in your industry.

Understand your customer persona

Your customer persona is a semi-fictional representation of who your ideal customer is. When you create a customer persona, you'll include information like demographics, behaviors, motivations, and goals. This helps you better understand who you're selling to and how to reach them. You can create a customer persona by conducting market research or surveys with current and potential customers.

Determine your revenue streams

The first step in creating your business model is to determine how you will generate revenue. There are numerous revenue streams you can explore, and the best way to determine which ones are right for your business is to research your industry and understand the market trends. Once you have a good understanding of the market, you can then choose the revenue streams that make the most sense for your business.

Some common revenue streams include advertising, subscription fees, product sales, and services. Depending on your industry, there may be other options as well. For example, if you're in the software industry, you may also want to consider licensing or freemium models.

Build your team

After you've determined how you will generate revenue, the next step is to build your team. This includes hiring employees, contractors, or freelancers who can help you with various aspects of your business. The size of your team will depend on the size and scope of your business. For example, if you're a small startup, you may only need a few employees or contractors to get started. However, if you're a larger company, you may need a more extensive team.

In addition to hiring employees or contractors, you also need to think about building partnerships with other businesses. This could involve anything from joint ventures to supplier agreements. Partnerships can be extremely helpful in growing your business and expanding into new markets.

Create your marketing strategy

Once you have a solid team in place, it's time to start thinking about marketing strategy. This includes figuring out what channels you will use to reach potential customers and what message you want to communicate through those channels. There are many different marketing channels available (online and offline), so it's important to choose the ones that are most likely to reach your target audience.

Your marketing strategy should also include a plan for measuring results so that you can track progress and adjust course as needed.

Some common marketing channels include social media, email, content marketing (blogging, infographics, etc.), paid advertising, and public relations. Again, the best way to determine which channels are right for your business is to research your industry and understand the market trends.

Once you have a good understanding of the market and your target audience, you can then create a detailed marketing strategy that includes specific goals, tactics, and timelines.

Essential components of an effective Business Plan

Executive summary

The executive summary is the first section of your business plan and should be written last. It's a brief overview of your entire business plan and should include your company's mission statement, an overview of your products or services, your target market, your competitive advantage, and a financial summary.

Company overview

This section of your business plan should provide an overview of your company, including its history (if any), structure (e.g., sole proprietorship, partnership, or corporation), management team, and location(s).

Products and services

This section should describe the products or services you offer in detail, including their features and benefits, pricing information, and any unique selling points. You should also include information on any patents or proprietary technology you have developed.

Market analysis

In this section of your business plan, you should provide an analysis of the market in which you will be selling your products or services. This should include information on the size and growth of the market, as well as any segments within it that you will be targeting. You should also discuss the competition in this market and how you will position yourself to compete effectively against them.

Sales and marketing strategy

Your sales and marketing strategy should outline how you plan to sell your products or services to your target market. This should include information on your distribution channels, promotional activities, pricing strategy, etc.

Get funding for your business

Before approaching potential investors, you need to have a clear understanding of how much money you will need to get your business off the ground or take it to the next level. This means creating a detailed financial forecast for your business. Your forecast should include:

-Start-up expenses: These are the one-time costs associated with getting your business up and running, such as legal fees, market research, and product development.

-Operating expenses: These are the ongoing costs associated with running your business on a day-to-day basis, such as rent, salaries, marketing, and inventory.

-Revenue: This is the money that your business will bring in through sales of products or services.

Once you have a good handle on your financial needs, you can start thinking about how to raise the money you need.

Create a pitch deck

A pitch deck is a presentation that entrepreneurs use to give potential investors an overview of their business and explain why they should invest in it. A well-crafted pitch deck should include:

An overview of the problem that your business is solving

An explanation of your solution

Information about your target market

Your business model

Your competitive landscape

Your team

Your milestones

Your financial projections

Approach investors

Now that you have a clear understanding of how much money you need and what you're going to use it for, as well as a pitch deck ready to go, it's time to start approaching potential investors.

When meeting with an investor for the first time, be sure to: Do your homework ahead of time and come prepared with questions about their investment history and what kinds of businesses they've invested in previously. Be clear about how much money you're looking to raise and what kind of equity you're willing to give up. Have a solid understanding of your business financials. Come across as confident but not cocky. Be able to articulate what makes your business unique and why you're going to be successful. Don't be afraid to ask for feedback, it can only help you improve your pitch down the line.

After the initial meeting, if an investor is interested in moving forward, they will usually request a copy of your business plan and financial projections. If everything looks good, they will then conduct due diligence, which is a process of investigating your business to confirm that the information you've provided is accurate and that your business is a good investment.

If all goes well and the investor decides to invest in your business, you will then negotiate and sign a term sheet, which is a document that outlines the key terms of the investment. Once the term sheet is signed, it's time to celebrate—you've just gotten funding for your business!

Creating a business plan is an important step for any entrepreneur. By taking the time to define your business, understand your industry, and develop a growth strategy, you can increase your chances of success. A well-thought-out business plan will give you the best chance of achieving your goals.

PART 3 – TEAM MANAGEMENT, OPERATING SYSTEMS, AND CASH FLOW

CHAPTER 10 - ORGANIZATIONAL STRUCTURE

When you launch your business, you need to establish an organizational structure that's not only effective but also efficient. You cannot scale your business if you do not have an Organizational Structure in your business.

An organization chart is a visual way of showing the relationships among people who work for the same organization. It shows how these people fit together in the company and what their roles are within it.

If you have a small organization with few employees, a simple structure might work best. But as the number of employees increases, it's essential to create formal roles and responsibilities so that everyone has their specific job tasks clearly defined. Doing so increases transparency and makes it easier to hire new employees and assign their roles.

An organizational structure affects every department in your business and every employee involved in any capacity. Structuring your business properly helps each employee operate more efficiently while making sure that all departments have clear reporting lines and know exactly what they should be doing on any given day.

Creating a business is all about making efficient use of time and resources, while also meeting the needs of customers and other stakeholders. An organizational structure is a way in which an organization divides tasks, departments, teams, and so on. Whether you're starting from scratch or need to revamp your business structure, this chapter will help you get organized.

Having a solid organizational structure can have a huge impact on how smoothly your company runs.

The organizational structure of your business determines how its departments operate and communicate with one another. A well-planned setup will not only streamline your team's operations but also prepare you for any future changes that may come along as your business grows.

Organizational effectiveness is a company's ability to achieve its goals and objectives. It is achieved by implementing an appropriate organizational structure, staffing it with competent employees, and providing them with the necessary resources.

An effective organizational structure is one that meets the company's goals and objectives while using its resources as efficiently as possible. Organizational structures are designed to make it easier to achieve organizational goals by making the most of the company's resources.

While there are many different types of organizational structures, you should carefully choose the one that best suits your business.

Benefits of Organizational Structures

An organizational structure has many benefits, including: -

Increased efficiency: An organizational structure makes it easier to determine which tasks will be done by which departments. This, in turn, makes it easier to assign and complete tasks. When tasks are completed more efficiently, the company saves time and money.

Increased productivity: By assigning tasks to the right people, a company will increase its productivity. It will be able to make more sales and increase its profit.

Improved staff satisfaction: When a company's organizational structure makes it easier to determine which departments handle which tasks, it also makes it easier for employees to know what they should be doing at any given time. This makes it easier for employees to know if they are meeting expectations.

Improved customer service: An organizational structure also helps with customer service. Ideally, it makes it easier to determine who manages customer complaints and who has the authority to make decisions that impact customers.

Increased innovation: An organizational structure can also help your company increase its ability to innovate. Organizing departments by function, for example, makes it easier to brainstorm new ideas.

Improved communication: An organizational structure also makes it easier to communicate with employees. This in turn makes it easier for employees to work together on projects that involve a lot of people and communicate effectively with one another about the project or task that involves a lot of people.

Improved decision-making: An organizational structure can also help your employees make better decisions. It can help them to determine which tasks to complete first. This will help them make better decisions, which will save time and money.

Improved accountability: As roles and job descriptions are clearly written for each position this will help your company hold employees accountable for their work and performance. This makes it easier for employees to know what they should be doing at any given time and what they should be working on next.

Increased profitability: An organizational structure can also help your company increase its profitability. For example, by assigning tasks to the right people, a company can increase its profitability by increasing its sales.

Delegation of duties: An organizational structure can also help your company improve its delegation of duties. For example, it can make it easier for managers to delegate certain tasks and responsibilities to employees.

Improved teamwork: An organizational structure can also help your company improve its teamwork. For example, it can make it easier for employees to work together on a project.

Standardization: Standardizing job descriptions and creating a standard organizational chart will make it much easier to determine who does what. This can help you avoid problems, such as employees trying to do jobs that don't fit them well.

Key elements of organizational structure

For creating the best organizational structure these are the key elements, you should consider:

Work specialization

One of the key elements of organizational structure is work specialization. This refers to dividing work into distinct activities, each of which is performed by a separate employee.

Work specialization is one of the key elements of organizational structure because it allows organizations to scale up their operations more easily. The earliest form of organizational structure is primitive specialization, which occurs when people choose to specialize in one task. Here each employee is assigned to specific duties that he specializes in based on his skills, qualification, and experience.

Departmentalization

Another key element of organizational structure is departmentalization. This occurs when an organization is divided into distinct departments, each of which performs a specialized set of activities. For example, an accounting department deals with all accounting activities. A sales department is responsible for all sales activities. A production department manufacture all company products. A marketing department develops all marketing campaigns. By dividing work into departments, you can ensure each function is appropriately fulfilled.

This is one of the key elements of organizational structure because it helps to reduce duplication in work. If one department handles multiple works, it'll be less efficient. A specialized department, on the other hand, has a clear set of tasks, and they don't need to worry about other departments.

Formalization

Organizational structure is also formalized. This occurs when an organization adopts a standard format for organizing its activities. For example, the accounting department has an organized structure that follows a specific format. The format is used to ensure all accounting activities are carried out in the same way, and that they're carried out efficiently.

This is one of the key elements of organizational structure because it ensures all employees perform their tasks in the same way.

If every employee has their own way of doing things, they'll be less efficient. A standard format or set of rules ensures all employees follow a set pattern, which makes them more efficient.

The organization's policies, procedures, guidelines, and rules are written for each position, so, that employees know what to do and how to do it. This rule book will be a guide for the employees in the organization.

Centralization and decentralization

Centralization and decentralization are two key elements of organizational structure because they affect how operations are managed.

Centralization refers to when decision-making authority is held by a central group (top-level management) inside the organization. Decentralization is when decision-making authority is held by a number of distinct groups within the organization. For example, in a centralized organization senior level employees takes all key decisions. In a decentralized organization, all levels of management contribute to decision-making.

Span of control

Another key element of organizational structure is the span of control. This refers to the number of employees a manager directly supervises. For example, a manager might have five employees.

A manager's span of control may be determined by the organizational chart. If a manager has a lot of employees to supervise, he may become less effective. Senior-level managers only oversee less number of employees (Middle-level managers and supervisors).

One common approach to organizational structure is to maintain a balance in the span of control as the level of the manager increases. This helps to simplify the chain of command.

Chain of command

The chain of command refers to the business hierarchy. The company's hierarchy is represented with an organizational chart. This ensures a clear direction for reporting by each employee. For example, an accounting manager may supervise two accountants, and he will report directly to the Chief Financial Officer (CFO). The CFO reports directly to the Chief Executive Officer (CEO). The CEO reports directly to the board of directors.

The chain of command is one of the key elements of organizational structure because it helps to simplify operations. It also helps managers monitor performance and identify bottlenecks.

Organizational structure gives a business its functioning structure. It refers to how an organization is structured to perform its functions and meet its goals. In other words, it's the way different departments within a company work together.

A well-designed organizational structure makes it easier for employees to do their jobs, and respond to changes in market conditions, new technologies, and customer preferences.

The key elements of organizational structure are work specialization, departmentalization, formalization, centralization and decentralization, the span of control, and the chain of command. These elements help to simplify operations and improve performance.

Types of Organizational Structures

In any business, the organizational structure you choose will have a significant impact on how your company operates and who has the final say in different operational decisions.

In order to find the best organizational structure for your business, it's important to understand all of your options first. With that in mind, there are many different organizational structures you can choose from when setting up your business.

Depending on what your company needs and the type of culture you want to establish, one of these structures may be a better fit for you than another.

These are the main structures that you can choose from:

Functional Structure

A functional structure organizes your business based on different functions or departments, such as marketing, finance, or human resources.

In a functional structure, each department is given its own set of goals and objectives, and a department manager oversees the employees of that particular department.

This organizational structure is very common, especially in small to medium-sized businesses. This structure is typically effective because each department has its own specific goals, objectives, and areas of responsibility, which makes it easier for individuals to know what's expected of them.

Divisional Structure

A divisional structure is very similar to a functional structure, except that it includes departments and functions that are broken down into smaller divisions based on specific geographies, products, or services.

Divisional structures are commonly used in large organizations that operate in a large geographical area or have thousands of products. Examples of the divisional structure are companies like Johnson & Johnson, McDonald's Corporation, Coca Cola.

Flat Structure

Also known as horizontal structure, used by many early-stage start-ups or small companies, here a lot of decision-making authority is given to employees without hierarchical pressures and there is no middle-level management.

Circular structure

Also known as horizontal structure, used by many early-stage start-ups or small companies, here a lot of decision-making authority is given to employees without hierarchical pressures and there is no middle-level management.

Network Structure

In Network Structure certain key functions are carried out by third-party vendors and contractors. For example, a food processing company uses a co-packer to manufacture their products, and distribute the products itself and it uses a marketing agency to market the product.

Organizational structure refers to how companies are structured, including the way they are broken down, the way they operate, and the relationships between employees.

Organizational structures are important because they give your organization a model and a blueprint for how things are run. Organizational structure is an important part of business management. It is crucial to understand the benefits of different organizational structures and how they can help maximize efficiency.

For businesses to be successful, it is important for them to have an organizational structure that is effective and efficient. The best organizational structure for your company will largely depend on the type of business you have, the size of your team, and your culture.

With so many different organizational structures available, it is important to understand which one will work best for your business. However, as you scale, remember it is equally as important to redesign your organizational structure to scale with the business.

CHAPTER 11 - STANDARD OF OPERATING PROCEDURES (SOPS)

Did you know that the majority of businesses fail because of human error? Or rather, a lack of attention to detail. In other words, many businesses fail simply because their team doesn't have the right processes in place to prevent these errors from happening.

If your business has failed recently or you see the potential for failure looming on the horizon, now is the perfect time to implement Standard Operating Procedures (SOPs). They are easy to overlook, but they are one of the most important aspects of any company, big or small.

At any given moment, there should be no doubt about what needs to be done in a given situation. It's easy to let details slip through the cracks when you're busy juggling new ideas and implementing strategies to stay ahead of the curve. A lack of standardized operating procedures can have serious consequences for your company.

Operating procedures are instructions or standards that guide employees in their day-to-day tasks. When standard operating procedures aren't in place, employee training is often inadequate, leading to a general decline in workplace efficiency.

A business is only as good as its employees, which means that every person on your team needs to be properly trained and equipped to do their job.

Standard operating procedures are the best way to provide this training. They are the ultimate guide for your employees, clarifying expectations and providing a roadmap for success.

They make onboarding new team members easier and more efficient, and they help prevent mistakes from occurring by accident. When implemented properly, standard operating procedures are a valuable asset for any business.

A standard operating procedure, or SOP, is a set of instructions that provides a step-by-step guide for completing a task. SOPs are created to help ensure consistency and quality in the performance of a specific task.

Standard operating procedures can be written for any number of tasks, from simple tasks such as how to properly answer the phone to more complex tasks such as how to troubleshoot a computer issue. In general, an SOP should include:

- The name or title of the procedure
- The person responsible for completing the task
- A step-by-step guide to completing the task
- Any relevant visuals or instructions

- The expected outcome of the task

The purpose of an SOP is to provide clear and concise instructions on how to complete a task. By having an SOP in place, you can be sure that everyone who needs to complete the task understands exactly what needs to be done and how it should be done. This can help improve efficiency and quality, while also reducing errors and inconsistencies.

An SOP can also serve as a training tool for new employees or for employees who need to refresh their memory on how to complete a particular task. Having all the steps laid out in one place makes it easier for someone to learn how to do something correctly.

Some of the business areas where SOPs are required are:
- Finance
- Production
- Team management - including hiring a new employee
- Marketing
- Sales
- Fulfillment
- After-sales service
- Each repetitive task

There are many benefits associated with creating and following standard operating procedures, including:

Smooth Operations: Standard operating procedures (SOPs) are important because they help ensure that an organization operates more efficiently.

It ensures that the organization is running smoothly and that its activities are conducted consistently and predictably. It helps to standardize processes.

It provides a set of guidelines for employees on how to carry out their duties and tasks, ensuring that everyone is operating within the same parameters.

Effective usage of resources: SOPs can help ensure that processes are followed correctly and that resources are used effectively.

Framework for an organization: Your organization needs a proper framework for operations. They provide guidelines for how an organization should operate. This ensures that operations are carried out consistently and efficiently, which can save time and money.

Improved quality control: By having clear and specific instructions on how something should be done, you can help ensure that it is done correctly every time. This can lead to improved product quality or service quality.

Increased efficiency: When everyone knows exactly what needs to be done and how it should be done, there is no wasted time or effort in trying to figure out what needs to be done next. This helps in improving efficiency, which ables your employees to perform at their highest level. This can lead to increased efficiency of your business and productivity overall.

Reduced costs: Having an efficient process in place can help reduce waste and rework, which can save your company money in the long run.

Improved safety: By having detailed instructions on how something should be done safely, you can help prevent accidents and injuries from occurring.

Standardization: Standard operating procedures are important because they help to standardize processes, which can improve communication and coordination between different parts of the business and get consistent outcomes. The operations are carried out in a consistent manner, which helps to achieve organizational goals.

How to create effective Standard operating Procedures?

Creating effective standard operating procedures is critical to the success of any organization. Whether it's a manufacturing company or a service organization, having well-defined and up-to-date procedures helps everyone know what needs to be done and how to do it.

While some businesses choose to develop their procedures internally, there are many benefits to working with an outside consultant who can bring fresh eyes and years of experience in developing successful SOPs.

Here are some tips for creating effective standard operating procedures:

1. Define the procedure's objective: Every SOP should have a clear purpose that supports the organization's goals and objectives. Be sure to include measurable goals so you can track the procedure's effectiveness over time.

2. Write a step-by-step outline: A good SOP will provide detailed instructions on every aspect of the procedure, from start to finish. Include visuals and diagrams whenever possible to help employees understand each step.

3. Make it user-friendly: An effective SOP is easy to read and understand. Use simple language and format the document in a way that makes it easy to follow. Avoid using jargon or acronyms that could confuse employees.

4. Revise and update regularly: As your business changes and grows, so too will your standard operating procedures. It is important to keep your SOPs up to date so that they can be used as an effective tool for running your business. If you find that

your SOPs are no longer accurate or relevant, be sure to revise and update them as soon as possible.

Be sure to review and update your SOPs regularly, at least once per year, to ensure they are still relevant and accurate.

Remember a standard operating procedure, or SOP is a set of step-by-step instructions that outline how to complete a task. SOPs are written to ensure consistency and quality in the performance of a specific task and to minimize variation and ambiguity.

Creating an effective SOP can be challenging, but it is essential to developing a successful business. By following the tips outlined above, you can create an SOP that will help your business run smoothly and efficiently.

CHAPTER 12 - CASH FLOW MANAGEMENT

Cash flow is an important part of any business. It is the measure of the operating cash to fund the ongoing activities of your business.

Cash flow means the movement of money into and out of the business.

The total amount of money received signifies inflow and all money spent signifies outflow.

Positive cash flow means when Cash inflow is greater than cash outflow.

Negative cash flow means when Cash outflow is greater than cash inflow.

Cash flow management is a process that monitors and manages your company's cash balance. It helps you understand how much cash your business has available at any given moment, as well as when more money will be coming in or going out again.

Cash flow management is the process of monitoring and maintaining an optimum balance between available cash and expenses.

Even the most profitable businesses can be affected by fluctuations in cash flow which make them vulnerable to going bankrupt if cash flow issues are not handled properly.

Around 66% of business owners fears that they will lose their business because of lack of available cash, if you have this fear you can eliminate it by implementing proper cash flow management.

To understand the importance of cash flow management, first, you need to know that your business consists of three types of cash flow activities:

- Cash Flows From Operating Activities: The amount of money a business generates (or consumes) through regular business operations such as manufacturing, selling products, providing a service to clients, paying expenses, etc. If left unmanaged, a business may find itself running out of operating cash and unable to fulfill short-term obligations and this will result in a negative impact on the performance of your business.

- Cash Flows From Investing Activities: The cash generated or invested as a result of investing activities. It tells us how much money was spent on (or earned by) investing during a certain period. Investing activities include the acquisition of physical assets, the purchase of securities, and the selling of securities or assets, etc.

- Cash Flows From Financing Activities: Cash flows from financing activities display the net cash flow utilized to fund the business. It is the net amount of funding generated by a business over a specific period. Finance operations include equity issue and buybacks, dividend payments, debt issuance, and repayment. Companies that require capital will raise funds through the issuance of debt or equity, which will be represented in the cash flow statement.

If you manage your cash flow well, you're more likely to succeed in business. The more cash you have available to meet your short-term obligations, the better prepared you are to stay in business for a long time.

While cash flow might not be the first thing you think about when you imagine running a successful business, it's one of the most important aspects of your operations.

Experts have identified cash flow management as one of the key drivers of business failure. This is because the majority of businesses are dependent on cash flow for their survival. This means that if you can't manage your cash flow properly, you're likely to go out of business.

A company's cash flow is a key performance indicator for businesses since it provides insight into how ready a company is to meet its short-term obligations.

Cash flow management also helps you identify where you might be able to reduce expenses or increase revenue by investing in the growth of your business.

Benefits of effective cash flow management

The benefits of effective cash flow management are vast and they extend to every aspect of your business. Some of the most prominent benefits of effective cash flow management include,

Reduction of financing costs: If your business has a low cash flow, you're likely to borrow money to fulfilling your operational costs and necessary expenses. However, if you manage your cash flow well, you'll be able to meet your business expenses without having to borrow money.

Reduction of risk: Being able to manage your cash flow well reduces the risk of business failure. This is because you're able to forecast your cash flow, spot any irregularities, and correct them before it's too late.

An increase in employee satisfaction: If you have a cash flow shortage you will not be able to pay salaries on time, but if you have enough cash flow for business operations and you pay employees salaries on time and pay them performance bonuses, they will be happy, and they're likely to stay with your team for a long time. This means that you'll have a loyal team with you that's more likely to contribute to your company's growth and success.

Less chance of bankruptcy: If you have a cash flow shortage and you run out of cash, you'll be in a position where you can't pay your bills on time. However, if you manage your cash flow well, you're less likely to have bankruptcy because your company will be able to pay its bills on time.

Increase in the value of the company: If you manage your cash flow well, it will increase the value of your company and make it more profitable. This is because it will allow you to invest more in growth and marketing activities that are essential for business success.

A better reputation: With a well-managed cash flow, people will trust your company. This means that your company will have a better reputation and be more likely to get the right people to work for you.

High growth rate: Being cash flow positive, helps you to grow faster. You will be able to hire more people and expand your operations into different markets and geographies.

3-month and 6-month Cash Flow Forecast

To ensure that your cash flow remains in check, it's important to forecast your cash flow over 3 months and 6 months. This will give you an insight into how much cash will be coming into the business, how much will be going out of the business, and when these expenses will be due. With this information, you can identify any irregularities and take steps to correct them before it's too late.

These forecasts help you better manage your cash flow. With this information, you can also identify areas in which you can cut down on expenses.

Cash flow management is the process of monitoring, controlling, and documenting cash to ensure that a business has the right amount at the right time to meet its ongoing obligations.

A company's cash flow is a key performance indicator for businesses since it provides insight into how ready a company is to meet its short-term obligations.

Cash flow management also helps you identify where you might be able to reduce expenses or increase revenue by investing in the growth of your business.

Part 4 - Marketing and Sales

CHAPTER 13 – CUSTOMER AVATAR

Creating a customer avatar is one of the first steps when creating an effective marketing strategy.

It's a common technique used in marketing, market research, and brand management.

A customer avatar is a visual representation of your ideal customer. It is a common marketing tool that simplifies customers' needs and wants. It is the easiest way to visualize who your ideal customer is and what they need from your product or service.

If you want to create a marketing strategy that will appeal to your customers, you first need to define who they are. To do that, you can create an avatar. It's a way of bringing these people to life so that you can get a better idea of what their needs and motivations are.

Why is creating a customer avatar important?

The process of creating a customer avatar helps you to understand your customers better, what their needs and wants are, how they think, and what they value. Based on this information you can tailor your marketing campaigns to appeal more specifically to that type of person, which will result in them being much more likely to respond positively to your campaign.

An avatar helps you understand your target customers better and come up with better solutions for them. It is an easy way to visualize who your customer is and
what they need from your product or service. It is a strategic tool that helps businesses simplify their customers' needs and wants while identifying potential opportunities to grow their business.

Determining your customer avatar Helps in your Content Marketing strategy, Paid Advertising, Product Creation, Copywriting, etc

When you know your target customers well, it will be much easier to create content that appeals to them. A customer avatar is essentially a profile of your ideal customer. It's a way of simplifying your customers' needs and wants so that you can better understand them.

How to create your Customer Avatar?

Define your customer: First, you need to define the type of customer you want to attract. You can do this by asking yourself questions, such as, who uses your product or service? What's their income and employment status? What are their motivations? Where do they live? What are their challenges?

Think about their needs: Once you know who your customer is, you can start thinking about their needs and challenges. This will help you to get a better idea of who your customer is and what they might be struggling with.

Visualize your customer: After that, you can visualize your customer. Visualizing your customer will help you to bring them to life and really get a better idea of who they are. You can do this by creating an avatar or a mock-up of your ideal customer.

Describe your customer: Once you have visualized your customer, you can describe them. Describe their likes, dislikes, pain points, hobbies, and personality. This will help you to paint a better picture and get a better idea of who your customer is and come up with better solutions for them.

Make sure the following points should be included in your customer avatar:

- Name
- Demographic - Age, sex, income, education, profes sion, family status, city
- Hobbies
- Fears
- Goals
- Ideals
- motivations
- Pain Points
- Views

Creating a customer avatar is an exercise to help marketers and business owners understand their ideal clients better. It's a way of bringing these people to life so that you can get a better idea of what their needs and motivations are. So that you can use this data for the betterment and success of your business.

CHAPTER 14 - 4 PS
OF MARKETING

The marketing process is so much more than just advertising your product or service and hoping that the right people would see it. Marketing is promoting your product or service in front of prospective customers.

It's an organized and systematic way to drive demand for your product or service by creating and implementing a plan that identifies potential customers, targets them based on their needs, and offers them the value they can't get anywhere else.

If you have a business or are thinking about starting one soon, learning about marketing will help you grow your customer base. Marketing is what brings your target customers to you.

It is also what helps your business continue growing after launch. Marketing is the key if you want to take your business to the next level!

Before we go further learning about marketing, let's see some different types of traditional marketing ways,

Print Marketing: Print marketing is the use of print media to promote a product or service. It includes newspapers, magazines, brochures, and other forms of printed media.

Direct Marketing: Direct marketing is the use of direct mail to promote a product or service. It includes letters, postcards, and other forms of direct mail.

Event Marketing: Event marketing is the use of events to promote a product or service. It includes conferences, trade shows, and other forms of events.

Outdoor Marketing: Outdoor marketing is the use of outdoor advertising to promote a product or service. It includes billboards, posters, and advertising on public transport such as buses, cabs, trains, etc.

Electronic Marketing: Electronic marketing is the use of electronic media to promote a product or service. It includes TV ads, radio ads, and other forms of electronic media.

What are the 4 Ps of Marketing?

The 4 Ps stand for product, price, place, and promotion. These are the core components of any marketing strategy. Understanding each of these components will help you design a marketing strategy that fits your business goals and objectives.

If you understand how these 4Ps interact and how each affects the outcome of a marketing campaign, you will be in a much better position to succeed than those who don't understand the basics of marketing.

Product

Product refers to the actual product or service you will offer. This is often the first thing potential customers will see, hear, or interact with.

Your product should match the needs and desires of your target customers. For example, if you have a vegan restaurant, your product would be vegan food. If your target customers are people who are concerned about their health, then offering tasty and healthy vegan food would make sense.

If your product doesn't match your customer's needs, then they probably won't buy it. The best way to think of your product is as a solution to a problem. Your target customers have a problem that they need to solve. And your product solves that problem.

The more specific you can be about the problem your product solves, the more attractive it will be to your customers.

Price

Price refers to the amount you charge for your product or service. The price of your product should reflect its value to customers. If people aren't willing to pay for your product, it won't matter how much advertising you do - your product won't sell.

If your product has a low perceived value, you'll need to either charge less for it or find a way to make customers think it's worth more. On the other hand, if your product has a high perceived value, you have the option of charging more for it.

There are several ways you can determine what price to set for your product. You could survey your target customers to see what they would be willing to pay. You could also use industry standards to determine if your product is priced too high or too low.

Keep in mind that you can always change your price. Just make sure you have a good reason for doing so like if you bring a new improved version of your product, you can charge more.

Place

Place refers to your distribution channel and where you sell your products or services. This is the method and channel through which your product gets from your company to your customers. For example, if you own a bakery, your place would be the bakery itself. If you own a yoga studio, your place would be the studio location. If you sell your products online at Amazon.com the place will be Amazon.com

Distribution channels can include direct sales, retail stores, online stores, pop-up shops, events, and more. Once you've identified your target customer, think about how you plan to reach them. If you're selling baked goods, you could sell them at your shop, farmers' markets, online, and/or hold baking classes at your house. If you're selling membership to your yoga classes, you could offer online yoga classes, hold yoga classes at yoga studios, and/or hold yoga classes in public places like parks. You have to consider where your customers are.

Promotion

Promotion refers to how you will bring attention to and advertise your product. This includes everything from the message you use to promote your product to the types of advertisements you run.

Successful promotion will entice customers to buy your product and drive them to purchase it from your distribution channel. There are tons of ways you can promote your product, but before you start putting effort into any one specific promotion strategy, you need to know who your customers are (that's why we create a customer avatar).

Once you've identified your potential customers, you can then decide which promotion methods would be most effective. Let's say you own a vegan bakery. Some ways you could promote your products include, hosting vegan baking classes, offering free vegan baked goods to local businesses, sponsoring events in your community related to health and wellness, creating and sharing recipes on your website, running ads on social media and in local magazines, etc.

Marketing isn't something you do once and forget about. It's something you do consistently, and it's something that must be an integral part of your business strategy.

If you don't understand and incorporate the 4 Ps into your marketing strategy, then you're missing out on one of the most effective ways to grow your business. To get the most out of your marketing efforts, be sure to follow the 4 Ps and remember that they must work together to create a cohesive strategy.

While one marketing method may work well, using only that method will only bring you so far. To drive results and make your marketing efforts as effective as they can be, you need to combine different marketing methods to reach your customers.

CHAPTER 15 - DIGITAL MARKETING STRATEGIES

I understand that creating a marketing strategy that works for your business might seem like a daunting task, but trust me, it doesn't have to be scary! The first thing you need to do is take a step back from all the noise and jargon, and identify who you are as a company and where you want to be in the future.

In the digital age, businesses must adapt to remain competitive. When marketing a business online, you must develop a strategy to stand out from your competitors and produce results.

A digital marketing strategy is essential for any organization looking to establish and maintain brand recognition among its target audience.

Digital marketing is a broad term for marketing your products or services online. Digital marketing allows businesses to reach customers in new ways and reach more people faster than ever before.

With so many digital platforms out there, it's easy to feel overwhelmed by the options available to you. But keeping things simple is key to any effective marketing strategy.

Digital marketing is an ever-evolving landscape of new practices, tools, and techniques. It's also an extremely fast-paced space with new trends emerging almost every day. This makes it challenging to keep your finger on the pulse of what's working best for your business and how to stay ahead of the game.

Keeping up with the latest digital marketing trends doesn't just help you stay ahead of industry changes — it also helps you identify which types of marketing are most effective for your business.

The Importance of Having a Digital Marketing Strategy

Marketing is all about connecting with your customers. Understanding their needs, wants and desires are essential if you want to create demand for your product or service.

A marketing strategy helps you ensure you're targeting your audience in the right way. It ensures you're spending your marketing dollars efficiently, and not just haphazardly throwing money into advertising in the hopes of bringing in new business.

A digital marketing strategy is all about reaching your audience through the channels they prefer to engage with. This can include everything from posting on social media to purchasing online advertisements, or even email marketing.

Having a digital marketing strategy in place will help you determine which channels are right for your business. It will also help you decide how to best utilize those channels to achieve your marketing goals.

Marketing your business online can be challenging, especially when you don't know which way would be the most effective. That's why it's important to have a digital marketing strategy in place.

A digital marketing strategy will help you determine which digital marketing tactics will be most effective for your business. It will also help you determine how to best utilize those tactics to achieve your business goals and objectives.

Having a digital marketing strategy in place will ensure you're reaching your audience in the right way.

Following are the steps involved in choosing the best tactics to incorporate into your digital marketing strategy:

Step 1: Define your business goals and objectives

Before you can identify the best digital marketing tactics for your strategy, you have to make sure you understand your goals and objectives as a business. What do you want to achieve as a company? Do you want to increase sales? Or do you want to increase brand awareness?

Depending on your business goals, you may want to focus on a different set of objectives. For example, if your goal is to increase sales, your objectives might be to increase average order value, increase the number of sales made per month, or increase the number of new customers.

Once you've defined your business goals and objectives, it becomes easier to identify which digital marketing tactics will help you achieve those goals.

Step 2: Understand your target audience

Every marketing campaign has a target audience. Understanding who you're marketing to will help you create an effective campaign and select the right digital marketing tactics. This will help you identify which digital platforms your audience spends time on.

Once you've identified your target audience, you can start to build a picture of who they are and what their needs, wants and desires are. This will help you create marketing messages that resonate with your audience and encourage them to take the next step and convert. As you have already created your customer avatar you can refer to that in this step.

Step 3: Research your competitors' digital marketing strategies

While this might not seem like it has anything to do with your brand's strategy, studying your competition can be incredibly insightful.

By analyzing your competitor's digital marketing strategies, You can learn about -

- What's working best in the industry

- Which marketing tactics are most effective in your industry
- You can learn about your audience
- What mistakes to avoid, You don't want to end up repeating the mistakes of your competitors and squandering your marketing budget in the process.

Step 4: Select the best digital marketing tactics for your strategy

Once you've gone through the process of defining your business goals and objectives, understanding your target audience, and researching your competitors' digital marketing strategies, you'll have a clearer idea of the best digital marketing tactics for your strategy.

Now is the time to take everything you've learned and identify the digital marketing tactics that will help you achieve your goals and objectives. Once you've selected the right digital marketing tactics for your strategy, it's time to put your plan into action.

There are several different digital marketing strategies you can use such as Affiliates, Influencer Marketing, Google Ads, Search Engine Optimization (SEO), Social Media Marketing (SMM), Email Marketing, and Content Marketing. We will look into each strategy one by one.

Affiliate Marketing

Creating an affiliate program for your business can be challenging. It requires a lot of hard work and dedication to making it successful. However, by using an affiliate program you can cost-effectively grow your business.

An affiliate program will enable you to reach out to potential customers on a much larger scale than before, through the help of other businesses that recommend or refer your services or products.

You will essentially be partnering with other businesses that would direct customers towards your business in exchange for a commission from sales that they drive to your site as a result of their recommendation or endorsement.

As an entrepreneur, you're always looking for new ways to grow your business. Working with affiliates can be an excellent way to expand your business and reach a new audience. These third-party partners help you drive sales and grow your brand by introducing it to their audience through partnerships they trust.

An affiliate program is a marketing strategy that enables you to partner with other businesses to promote your products or services. Affiliates include bloggers, social media influencers, and other businesses that earn a commission by referring customers to you.

For example, if you own a website that sells T-shirts, an affiliate program would allow other sites to refer their visitors to your site. In return, these affiliates would get a percentage of the sale's profit, when the customers that they referred to your site make a purchase.

Typically affiliates already have an audience and want to expand their business by partnering with other businesses. They're likely to have existing relationships and the trust of their audience. Their audience values their opinion and is more likely to take positive action when they send them to your site. You can also use affiliates to increase brand awareness apart from driving sales.

Affiliate marketing is effective and can help you add new

customers and generate more sales. If you want to attract new customers and increase sales, an affiliate program might be for you.

Here are a few reasons why affiliate marketing can help you grow your brand and expand your business:

Affiliate marketing helps you market to new audiences: By partnering with affiliates, you can market to new audiences to that you don't have access. Affiliates have a variety of reach as they might have their online communities, such as Facebook groups or blogs, and they might have an audience to that you don't have access. By using affiliates, you can increase your audience and expand your reach.

Affiliate marketing is cost-effective: Affiliate marketing is a cost-effective way to grow your business because you're not paying for marketing. You will only pay Affiliates if they bring sales. You are not paying affiliates any money upfront.

Affiliate marketing is scalable: Affiliate marketing is a scalable strategy that can help you grow your business faster. You can partner with multiple affiliates to expand your reach by attracting new audiences.

Low risk: Affiliate marketing is not risky. You don't have to make payments to the affiliates unless there are conversions.

Brand Building: Brand building is the process of creating a brand identity and building a brand image. You can use affiliate marketing to build your brand and brand image by partnering with affiliates to market your products or services. Affiliates can help you build your brand reputation by promoting your products or services.

There are some steps you can take to select the right affiliates and run an effective affiliate program. Here are a few things you should keep in mind to grow your business through affiliate marketing.

Define your goals: Before you jump into creating an affiliate program, it's important to define your goals. Why do you want to create an affiliate program? What will the program look like? How will it work? What are your key performance indicators?

Create your marketing materials: Once you've defined your goals, you can start creating marketing materials that are appropriate for your affiliates. You can create your landing pages, product pages, email templates, display ads images, and sales funnels.

Find the right affiliates: When you're building an affiliate program, you should start by finding the right affiliates. You can do this by asking your existing customers which online communities they visit and which social media influencers they follow. You can also join an affiliate network and which will help you to bring in affiliates to your affiliate program. Each industry has different affiliate networks, just search Google. Major Affiliate networks are Clickbank, commission junction, ShareASale, MaxBounty, JvZoo, Rakuten Marketing, etc.

Establish clear terms and conditions: Once you've found the right affiliates before you begin to work with them, it's important to establish clear terms and conditions. Affiliates are essentially your partners so it's important to set clear expectations so you can avoid any miscommunications or misunderstandings.

Keep track of your affiliates' progress: Once you've recruited affiliate partners and established terms and conditions, you should keep track of their progress and success. You should be able to track your affiliate's performance. If you join any affiliate network and list your product they will provide affiliate tracking.

Be consistent with your communications: Regularly communicate with your affiliates. Stay consistent with the way you communicate and let affiliates know when you've updated your marketing materials. Stay consistent with your communications to make sure your affiliates feel engaged and know they're an important part of your business.

Affiliate marketing can be a great way to spread your brand and attract new customers. If you're an entrepreneur, building an affiliate program can be an excellent way to grow your business, expand your reach, and generate more sales.

Influencer Marketing

Influencers are individuals who have a large, loyal following such as bloggers, youtube video creators, celebrities, or famous social media influencers. Influencers have followers who listen to them and follow their advice about products or services.

People trust influencers, they will buy products that are recommended by influencers as compared to products from random advertising. As a result, brands are collaborating with top-tier social media influencers so they can reach their potential customers and drive sales of their products.

An influencer could be anyone from your best friend with 1,000 followers to a YouTube star with millions of subscribers.

The digital marketing world is constantly changing and evolving, creating new opportunities for brands. Influencer marketing has become one of the most popular forms of digital marketing for business that wants to reach the masses.

Influencer marketing is fast becoming one of the most effective ways to reach your target audience. It involves working with social media influencers — also known as "digital influencers" or "online personalities"— to collaboratively market your brand, product, or service.

It helps you tap into their audience by reaching out to influencers who have a dedicated following in your niche. With the right strategy, you can use influencer marketing to create positive buzz about your brand and drive sales.

Influencer marketing is a form of marketing where you sign up and work with social media influencers to promote your brand. By tapping into the networks of these social media stars, you can increase sales of your product or service.

Brands can use influencer marketing to boost awareness, increase brand loyalty and drive sales by using the followers of social media personalities. There are many advantages to using influencer marketing to promote your products and services. These include,

Brand awareness: If people see your product featured by influencers, they become aware of your brand and start to recognize your logo.

Audience growth: If your product is featured by a popular influencer, their followers see the post and be interested in purchasing it. This can increase your overall audience and lead to more sales in the future.

Increased engagement: People are more likely to engage with your brand if they've seen it recommended by a social media influencer. This can result in more sales and increased revenue for your business.

How to build a thriving influencer marketing campaign?

Before you start working with influencers, it's important to plan out your campaign and determine what you want to achieve. This will help you stay focused and determine which influencers would be a good fit for your brand.

Some of the best practices you should follow to ensure you're getting the most out of this marketing strategy,

Define your goals: What are you hoping to achieve with your influencer marketing campaign? Are you hoping to drive brand awareness or increase sales? Once you know what your goals are, it will help you find the right influencers.

Find the right influencers: Identify the best influencers for your brand and product. Decide which social media channel you want to focus on. Then, look for the most relevant influencers for that channel. This will help you reach your target audience and make an impact.

Be selective: You don't want to work with just any influencer. Instead, make sure you're working with the best influencers who will help you reach your target audience.

Audience and demographics: Look for influencers who have a large, engaged audience that matches your target demographic. This will help you reach your ideal customers and make an impact.

Engagement: You want to work with influencers who can engage their audience and get them excited about your brand. This will help you drive sales and make an impact on potential customers.

Relevance to your brand: Make sure the influencers you choose are relevant to your brand and product. This will help you drive more sales.

Create a budget: Depending on the type of influencer you want to work with, this type of marketing can relatively cost thousands of dollars. Make sure you create a budget so you know how much you can spend on this campaign.

Create a campaign plan: Once you've found the right influencers, create a campaign plan to help you stay focused. This will help you create a detailed strategy for your campaign.

Use a contract: Once you've found the influencers you want to work with and have created a campaign plan, use a contract to outline the terms of your partnership. This will help you protect your brand and make sure the influencers follow through on their end of the deal.

Keep track of results: Track the results of your influencer marketing campaign to see if it's effective. This will help you determine if you should continue using it or if you should try something different.

When done right, influencer marketing can be an extremely effective strategy for promoting your brand or product.

It's important to find the right influencers and create a strong partnership with them. This will help you reach your target audience, boost brand awareness and drive more sales.

To make the most of influencer marketing, you need to have a clear idea of who your target audience is and how you want to reach them. Then, you need to find social media influencers who have a significant following in your desired niche.

You can use influencer marketing to create positive buzz about your brand and increase your business.

Google Ads

Google ads are a great way for your business to build visibility and generate leads. But with so many different kinds of Google ads available, it can be difficult to know which advertising option is the best one for your business.

You may not be using Google ads until now because most businesses find them to be too expensive. However, if you approach them from the right angle, they can be a very effective way to bring in new customers.

Google Ads (previously known as Google AdWords) is a search engine advertising service from Google that allows advertisers to place ads on Google, and its partner websites, as well as video advertisements on YouTube.

It allows businesses to reach users based on their needs and interests through advertisements. However, with so many different features, it can quickly become overwhelming for new users.

With Google Ads, users can create and manage advertisements through a tailored search network or display network. If you are thinking of starting a new business or expanding an existing one by adding new products, services, or markets - Google Ads could be one of the perfect options for you.

Google Ads connects advertisers to customers who search for products and services on Google.

It's a cost-per-click bid auction system that helps businesses advertise their website and services on Google search results, YouTube, and on other partner websites.

When you create an ad, you choose where to show your ad [placement], how much you're willing to spend, and your ad copy. Your ad can show on Google search results, YouTube videos, Gmail, and other partner sites.

Google Ads bidding works as follows: Advertisers create an ad with a certain bid amount. Google then determines which ad gets featured on top of the search results based on relevance and the bid amount. The advertiser who is willing to pay the most for that ad spot gets the top spot. Once an ad is clicked, the advertiser is charged the bid amount for that ad.

Key Things to Know Before Starting Your Google Ads Campaign

Understanding your customers: Before you start creating ads, you need to understand your customers and their needs.

Competitor research: You can also do competitor research to find out what types of ads they are running and what their marketing strategy is. You can use tools like Spyfu to learn more about your competitors' Google Ads.

Knowing what you want to achieve: Do you want to generate brand awareness or increase your website traffic? Do you want to drive people to your store or sell services online? Google Ads allows you to choose from a variety of campaign types, including video, text, or images. You can also set daily budgets and track your performance to see what's working and what's not.

Choosing the right keywords: Google Ads provides a variety of keyword options that you can use to target different audiences. It's important to know who your target audience is and what they're interested in so you can create a campaign that will work most effectively. For example, if you're running a campaign for an e-commerce store, you'll want to target keywords like "apparel" or "clothing."

Choosing the right ad type: Google Ads allows you to choose between different ad types. You can choose text ads, image ads, video ads, and other types. They all work in the similar way.

Choosing the right bid: Google Ads allows you to set a bid (or maximum bid) for your ad. For example, if you want to run an ad that shows up on the first page of Google search results, you'll want to set a max bid [this can be seen in the keyword research tool 'keyword planner' provided by google]. This lets advertisers know how much they should pay per click for their ads, and it also allows them to control their own budgeting process. Each keyword has a max bid. Search for keywords that you want to target and then set the maximum bid for your ad. You can also increase or decrease your max bid based on your results or the results of other advertisers.

Campaign Objective: You can set the objective for your campaign, which will help you determine the type of ads you should be running. By setting an objective, you can tell Google what type of ad you want to show up on the search results page, along with how much you'll pay per click. Campaign Objective includes - Sales, Leads, Website Traffic, Product and Brand Consideration,

Brand Awareness and Reach, App Promotion, Local store visits, and promotions.

Let us see some of the tips that you can use while creating your Google Ads copy -

Ad Headline: Your ad headline should be very clear and concise. It should tell people what's in it for them and why they should click. Avoid using common words like "free," "sale," or "new." To increase ad relevancy Include your Keyword in Headline.

Ad Body: The ad body should have a brief description of your product or service, what it does, and why people should buy it. You can also include special offers and discounts.

Call To Action: Your ad's call to action should tell people what to do next. You can use words like "click here," "sign up," "shop now," or "learn more."

Google Ads is one of the most powerful advertising platforms that help businesses make more money with less effort. With the right know-how and tools, setting up your account does not have to be complicated and time-consuming.

SEO

Google is the world's leading search engine with an 80%+ market share. As a result, Google search has a tremendous impact on user behavior, which impacts how users discover websites and conduct their online searches.

Furthermore, given that most of us spend a lot of time using search engines to find information or look up products and services, it's no surprise that search engines have grown to become such an essential part of our online lives.

Since its first beta release in 1998, Google Search has come a long way. Google Search is the key to unlocking the untapped potential for your website traffic and visibility.

Search engine optimization (SEO) is a technique to improve your website's ranking in search engines like Google, Bing, and Yahoo.

Search engine optimization (SEO) can be a tricky beast to tackle. It's also one of the most challenging marketing disciplines you can take on as an entrepreneur. If you aren't careful, SEO has the potential to backfire and hurt your brand.

However, if you implement it correctly, it can drive massive amounts of organic traffic(for which you don't pay anything/free traffic) to your website and help increase conversions.

Search engine optimization (SEO) refers to the process of increasing the visibility of a website or a blog by managing the way the site or blog is delivered or represented, in the results of a search engine.

When people use a search engine to find something online, they don't just type in one word. Instead, they type in a phrase with several words in it. This is known as a keyword or a keyphrase.

If you want your website to show up in a high position on the list of search results, then you need to optimize your site for search engines.

If your website doesn't show up in the top 5 results for a particular keyword, potential customers may never find your site. It's not enough to write great content. You also need to make sure that search engines can find it.

The art of keyword research

Keyword research is one of the most important aspects of SEO.

However, many brands spend months creating content only to discover that their target audience isn't even seeing it. That's because they forgot to consider the significance of SEO.

The reality is, ranking high on search engine results is critical to the success of your website. You might have the best content in the world, but if it isn't visible, it's not doing you any good. That's where keyword research comes in.

The first step of keyword research is to determine what you want to rank for. Then, you'll want to select a few keywords that are most relevant to your product.

Keep in mind that the keywords you choose should also have a high search volume. Otherwise, you're setting yourself up for failure. To find out how many people are searching for certain keywords each month, you can use tools like Google's Keyword Planner or Ahrefs.

On-Page SEO

On-page SEO is optimizing certain components of a webpage which includes optimizing the title, URL, meta description, anchor text, internal links, author box, etc.

Title: The title of your blog post or article is what shows up in the search engine results, so it's important to include your target keyword in the title.

URL: The URL of your blog post or website page should include the keyword as well.

Meta Description: Your meta description is another critical aspect of on-page SEO, it is the snippet of text that appears below the title in search engine results. It's important to use your target keyword in your meta description as well. Your meta description is also a critical factor for bringing people to your website.

Off-Page SEO

The next part of SEO to consider is off-page SEO. This refers to any action you take to increase the authority of your website or blog in the eyes of search engines. Off-page SEO is often overlooked, but it has a big impact on your search engine rankings.

There are many different things you can do to increase the authority of your website. It can be as simple as creating a social media campaign that drives traffic to your blog. It can be guest blogging, reaching out to influencers in your industry, republishing your content, or creating a resource that other bloggers in your space would want to link to.

It's vital to understand these important points of off-page SEO,

1. Link building: This refers to creating links pointing to your website or blog from other websites or blogs. In general, this should be permitted for any site that has a good amount of traffic, but it's important to note that Google frowns upon many link-building methods as they are considered spammy. Instead, link building should be limited to sites with high authority, relevance, and quality content related to your business or topic.

2. Backlink analysis: This refers to a process where you analyze the links pointing to your site and to your competitors' sites to determine the quality of these links and the link gap.

3. Social media: This refers to all the social media platforms you use for your marketing, including Facebook, Twitter, LinkedIn, Reddit, etc. You have to place your website link on all social media accounts of your business.

4. Citations: This is important for Local SEO. Citations are the reference of your website containing the business name, address, and phone number (NAP). Citations are manually built on websites such as Yelp, Yellow Pages, Google Business Profile, Bing

Maps, etc.

5. Press Release: Press Release is important for branding as well as for link building. You may need to purchase PR every 28 days because major news websites delete their old content every 28 days cycle.

SEO Mistakes to Avoid

Manipulating Rankings: Don't try to manipulate your rankings. This is a common mistake of people who don't truly understand SEO. It's important to understand that rankings, and the algorithms that Google uses to determine them, are based on a set of rules. These rules are designed to measure how many links a page has from other websites. You shouldn't be trying to trick search engines, as this will not bring you long-term benefits.

Thin Content: This is a common mistake that people make when it comes to writing content. What I recommend is to search your keyword in Google, check the top 10 listings, and note down the number of words they have written on that particular topic, after that take the average and you will exactly know how many words should be included in the content that you need for that particular keyword.

Link building in Bulk: One of the biggest mistakes you can make is to build links in bulk. You should never purchase links through platforms like Fiverr, there are a number of sellers that provide thousands of links for $5, this is totally unnatural and Google can see it. Usually, natural link building is a visitor comes to your site, finds relevant content, he mentions your content with a link on his site. What we do in our Agency is manually outreach reputed blogs for getting links for our clients.

Keyword Stuffed Content: This is a very common mistake in SEO.

You do not want to be the site that has keyword-stuffed content. Search engines will not rank your site for a keyword if it contains the same keyword too many times. What I recommend is to use at most 2 times a particular keyword every 500 words.

Not Updating your Old Content: One of the problems that I see with most websites is their content is out of date, they are not updating their content and it's getting old. It's not good to have a website that is out of date or has old content. You need to update your content, it needs to be fresh and fresh content is what Google loves.

Not Adding New Content: Depending on your niche, you need to add new content. If you are in a local business add at least one article every 2 weeks.

Duplicate Content: Duplicate content is content that is copied from some other website. For example, if you have a website and you copy the same article from some blog, then your content is duplicated and your site is going to be penalized by search engines. Duplicate content does not add any value to your site. Even if you take some parts of content from another's article and put it on your website as it is, it is still considered duplicate content.

Social Media Marketing

Today, businesses that ignore social media marketing are at risk of losing the loyalty of their customers and diminishing brand visibility. Social media marketing is a strategy that helps businesses grow by staying connected with their audience and potential customers on social networks.

These sites are a great way to connect with people who might be interested in your business or services. They can also be an effective way to drive new visitors to your website or blog and offer another avenue for word-of-mouth advertising.

Social Media Marketing is an online marketing technique through which companies can organically reach or advertise their products directly to potential customers on different types of Social Media Platforms such as Facebook, Twitter, TikTok, Instagram, etc.

Because there are so many social platforms out there these days, it's important for you to know which one is right for you and which ones you should avoid.

Social media marketing is an incredibly cost-effective form of brand building. It doesn't require a huge advertising budget. Rather, it's a way to create content that's valuable to your audience and get people talking about you.

One of the biggest benefits of social media marketing is that it's a way to increase awareness of your brand. It's also a way to increase engagement with your current customers. By encouraging customers to become brand advocates, you can greatly increase your reach.

Social media also allows you to have a two-way conversation with your audience, which allows you to gather feedback, find out what your customers want, and become more transparent.

Which social media platform is right for your business?

When it comes to picking which social media network(s) to invest your time, money, and energy in, it's important to choose the ones that align with your business goals and target audience.

It's also helpful (and more realistic) to pick one or two social media networks to start with and then expand your marketing strategy from there. If you try to take on too many social media networks at once, you run the risk of spreading yourself too thin and seeing little to no results.

Here are a few things to keep in mind when determining which social media network(s) are right for your business: -

Existing customer base: Where are your customers primarily spending their time online? If they're all on Facebook, it might be a good idea to focus your efforts there. If they're split between Facebook, Twitter, Instagram, and a few other networks, you might want to consider diversifying your social media efforts.

Target customers: Who are your target customers and what social networks do they spend their time on? If you sell products or services geared toward a younger audience, you'll likely want to focus on Snapchat, Instagram, and maybe even TikTok. If your customers are mostly middle-aged and above, you might want to focus more time on Facebook, Twitter, and LinkedIn.

Business goals: What are your short-term and long-term business goals? What do you want to accomplish with your social media marketing efforts? If you're new to social media marketing, start with one network and then expand your efforts when you feel more comfortable. If you want to see immediate results, you might want to focus your efforts on networks like Facebook and Instagram. If you want to create long-term relationships with your customers, you might want to consider networks like Twitter and LinkedIn.

Some tips for your Social Media Marketing

Spend time on your brand's profile
First and foremost, think about the amount of time you have to

post and take full advantage of it. The average Instagram post is just under two minutes. Although you can't post 24/7, don't post less than once every 24 hours on any platform. If you're not posting daily, then people will forget about you and what you do.

Besides posting regularly, there are a few other things you can do to ensure your social media strategy is successful. Ensure your social media profiles are filled out, including your website and email address if applicable. Update your social media images to add your logo and include your company's tagline.

Post your content at optimal timing

One of the best ways to maintain engagement and make your followers interact with your post is through your content's timing. There are a few social media platforms that don't allow you to choose a date and time, but on others, you can choose when you want to publish your content.

Timing your content can help boost engagement and create a more engaged following by forcing your followers to interact with your posts. While creating your content, think about how you want your followers to respond to your posts. Do you want them to like and comment on your posts?

Show you care by responding to comments and questions

Showing you care for your followers is key to creating a loyal base of brand advocates. If people feel that you care about them, then they're more likely to become advocates for your brand.

One way to show you care is by responding to comments and questions. This can show your followers that your brand truly cares about their needs.

If someone comments on your post and asks a question, then you have two options -

Option one is to reply to and address the question directly, which shows your followers you care about their needs and will address any concerns.

Option two is to simply ignore the comment, but be aware that this will negatively impact your social media presence.

I always recommend not hiding or avoiding answering any questions about your brand. This can come off as dishonest, and it will likely result in fewer followers seeing your social media posts and less engagement.

Don't be afraid to ask for feedback

The best social media strategies, especially ones that involve marketing, are constantly evolving and improving. Therefore, you should never be afraid to ask your followers what they think of your brand and how you can improve your social media strategy.

Remember, always be open and honest with your followers when asking for feedback.

Form an online community by giving back

The best social media strategies involve more than just posting content. You can't just post content and expect your followers to interact with it. It takes effort and time to interact with your followers, and you can't do it by yourself.

Therefore, be sure to involve your audience in your social media strategy by allowing them to help create and post content. Setting up a social media community can be challenging, especially if you don't have a dedicated individual who manages your community.

Be consistent with your posting schedule

The social media strategies that work best are the ones that are consistently used. Therefore, the best social media strategies are the ones you use on a daily basis.

Social media platforms are constantly updating their algorithms, and the way you post on one platform may not work on another. The best way to ensure that you succeed with your social media strategy is to post content on a daily basis.

The more often you post, the more likely your followers are to see your social media content. Even if the content isn't perfect, it's better than being posted once every few weeks.

Use visual content to stand out from the crowd

One of the best ways to create engaging social media strategies is by using visual content. Visual content is images and videos, and you can use them to stand out from the crowd on social media platforms.

Visual content is great because it allows you to create engaging content without needing to write long blog posts. Instead, you can create visual content that focuses on action, such as images of people using your product.

Show, don't just tell, with your brand's content

The best social media strategies will be successful if they are consistently used. The best way to ensure this happens is by showing your followers on social media what your brand stands for, not just telling them.

Your brand's social media content can have a big impact on your social media strategy and your brand's success. It's important to remember that the social media posts you create are a reflection of your company, so make sure they reflect the values and personality of your brand.

Take the time to think about what your brand stands for and create content that embodies this brand personality. Make sure your social media content is authentic, genuine, and reflects what your brand is.

Social media has become an essential tool for many brands, and there are many ways to approach your social media strategy. The tips and strategies discussed above will help you create an engaging social media strategy for your brand.

The best social media strategies are the ones that are consistently used. Social media strategies don't work if they're only used occasionally. The more often you post, the more likely your followers are to see your social media content and the more likely they are to interact with your brand.

These tips will help you create an engaging social media strategy for your brand. The key is to use social media in a way that reflects your brand's values and personality.

Social media marketing isn't a trend that will die out soon; it's a marketing strategy that continues to grow and evolve as new platforms emerge and existing ones change or update their platforms.

It's important for businesses to stay on top of trends and understand how social media is evolving so they can best use the platforms and make the most of their marketing strategy.

Once you choose the social media platforms that are right for your business, it's time to get started with your marketing strategy. It may take some time to see results from social media marketing, but you'll be glad you made the effort when you do.

Email Marketing

Email marketing is a strategy that involves sending emails to your customers or potential customers [people who may be interested in your products or services]. E-mail is still one of the most effective ways to get in front of your target audience.

With email marketing, you can convey your message at any time. You can promote new content or offers at any given time of the year, depending on what's relevant for your audience at that particular time.

You can set up an email marketing campaign to promote your products and services to engage with your audience, or even to increase brand awareness.

You can either do extensive research, or you can base your campaign on what your past/current customers have told you about their experience with your products or services.

You can also use email as a way to stay connected with your customers who are interested in your products. Unlike social media, email marketing stays in people's inboxes, where it can be viewed at any time.

You can use email for collecting feedback about your products and services or for keeping your customers updated about new content from your company.

You can let your customers know about special offers, discounts, and other promotions that may be of interest to them. Email marketing can also help you improve customer retention by providing an easy way for your customers to contact you with any questions or issues they might have.

Email also allows you to easily segment your subscribers based on their interests, so you can send highly targeted messages to each group. This allows your company to reach a larger audience while still providing a personalized experience for each subscriber.

Email marketing can be a great way to reach out to your target audience and promote your product or service. However, it's important to create an effective email marketing campaign in order to get the most out of your efforts.

Plan Your Campaign

Define Your Objective

Before you launch your email marketing campaign, you need to take a step back and think about what you want to achieve with your emails. Do you want to increase brand awareness? Drive traffic to your website? Generate leads? Convert customers? Once you know your objective, you can start planning your campaign accordingly.

Choose the Right Email Service Provider

There are a lot of email service providers out there, so it's important to choose one that fits your needs. If you're just starting out, you may want to go with a free or low-cost option like MailChimp or Constant Contact. But if you're looking for more features and advanced reporting, you'll need to invest in a premium provider like HubSpot or Pardot.

Build Your Email List

Your email list is one of the most important assets of your email marketing campaign. Without a good list of subscribers, your chances of success are slim to none. There are a few different ways to build your list, including buying lists, renting lists, and growing lists organically through opt-ins and sign-ups.

Create Your Email Template

Once you have your email list and service provider set up, it's time to create your email template. This will be the foundation for all of your emails moving forward, so it's important to get it right from the start. There are a few things to keep in mind when creating your template: make sure it's mobile-friendly, use branding elements (like logos and colors), and include an obvious call-to-action (CTA).

Write Compelling Content

Your subject line is your first (and maybe only) chance to make a good impression, so don't take it lightly! Keep your subject lines short, sweet, and to the point. Make sure they accurately reflect the content of your email and avoid using misleading "bait" subject lines that will disappoint recipients when they open your email.

To write effective subject lines, start by thinking about what would make you want to open an email. What are some of your favorite subject lines? Some common themes include:

- Asking a question
- Making a promise
- Using humor
- Including a number or statistic
- Using provocative language

No matter what approach you take, make sure your subject line is clear and direct. Avoid cute puns or complex wordplay that might not translate well. And always proofread your subject lines before sending!

One way to make your emails more compelling is to personalize them as much as possible. Include the recipient's name in the subject line and in the body of the email whenever possible.

You can also segment your list so that you can send more targeted emails based on factors like location, age, gender, etc. The more relevant and personalized your emails are, the more likely people are to engage with them.

Most people are busy and have limited time to read emails, so it's important to keep your content concise and to the point. Get straight to the point in the opening sentence or two, and use clear language throughout.

Use bullet points or numbered lists whenever possible, and break up large blocks of text with headings and white space. And don't forget to proofread your emails before sending them.

Timing Is Everything

When it comes to email marketing, timing is everything. You need to find the right frequency for your campaign in order to keep your subscribers engaged without bombarding them with too many emails. The best way to do this is to start slow and gradually increase the frequency as you go.

Once you've found the right frequency for your campaign, it's important to test, test, and test some more. Try sending emails at different times of the day or week and see how your subscribers respond. Pay attention to open rates and click-through rates to get an idea of what works best for your audience.

Email marketing can be a great way to connect with your audience and promote your business or product. However, it's important to plan and execute your campaign carefully in order to achieve success.

Measure Your Results

To measure the success of your email marketing campaign, you need to track two key metrics: open rate and click-through rate (CTR).

Open rate is the percentage of people who open your email. A good open rate is between 15-25%.

The Click-through rate is the percentage of people who click on a link in your email. A good CTR is between 2-5%.

There are a few different ways to track opens and clicks:

Most email service providers (ESPs) will track this data for you and provide reports on it. This is the easiest way to track opens and clicks, but it's not always 100% accurate.

You can also add tracking parameters to your links using Google Analytics or other tracking tools. This is more accurate than relying on ESP reports, but it's also more complicated.

If you're not sure which method to use, start with ESP reports and then switch to tracking parameters if you want more accurate data.

Once you've been tracking opens and clicks for a while, you need to start analyzing your results to see what's working and what isn't.

Here are a few things to look at,

Open rate: Are people opening your emails? If not, why not? Try changing your subject lines or sending more relevant content.

Click-through rate: Are people clicking on your links? If not, why not? Try changing the placement of your links or making them more relevant to your readers.

Unsubscribe rate: Are people unsubscribing from your emails? If so, why? Try changing the frequency of your emails or the type of content you're sending.

Complaint rate: Are people marking your emails as spam? If so, why? This could be a sign that you're sending too many emails or that your content is irrelevant.

Below are some of the most common mistakes in email marketing. Be sure to avoid these so that you can improve your campaign's overall effectiveness:

- Sending too many emails
- Not segmenting your email list
- Not giving customers a way to opt-out
- Not including a clear call to action
- Sending irrelevant emails
- Not optimizing your emails
- Using a bad email marketing platform

You should now have a good understanding of how to create an effective email marketing campaign. By following the tips mentioned above in this post, you can make sure your campaign is successful.

Email marketing has been the top communication channel for businesses for a long time, and it continues to thrive in the modern digital world.

To build an effective email marketing strategy, you need to create a detailed plan that outlines your goals, audience, and objectives. Once your plan is in place, you can start to incorporate email into your marketing strategy.

Finally, remember that email marketing works best when it's targeted, so take the time to segment your email lists based on interests and preferences so that you can craft more personalized messages.

Content Marketing

Content marketing is one of the strategies by which businesses reach their potential customers online.

Content marketing is quickly becoming the go-to marketing strategy for brands looking to establish a stronger relationship with current customers and drive brand awareness among prospective buyers.

Before we dive into the specifics of how content marketing works, it's helpful to define what content marketing actually is.

In its most basic form, content marketing is the process of creating and distributing content that your target audience wants to read, listen or watch and it is a proven way to make your brand seem trustworthy and help you stand out from the competition. The goal is to attract new customers and increase awareness of your brand.

Content marketing can be in many forms like blogs, podcasts, ebooks, webinars, youtube videos, social media posts, etc.

The key to content marketing is understanding your audience. Content marketing requires that you think strategically about what types of content will appeal most to your target audience and how it will best serve their needs.

You need to know what your target customers care about, what they're interested in, what problems they need to be solved, what questions they have, and what their lifestyle is like. Once you know this information, the next step is to use it to create content that addresses their needs.

The content that you choose can be of different forms, depending on your industry. For example, if you're in the fitness industry, your content might take the form of workout videos. If you're in the travel space, it might take the form of city guides.

Creating content is important for any business, but content marketing is especially important for businesses that are just getting off the ground. Do you know businesses that use content marketing grow two times faster than those that don't.

When you create content, you're establishing yourself as an authority and helping potential customers solve their problems. You're also increasing your brand's exposure and building trust — which in turn leads to more conversions and sales.

How to Create Great Content for your Content Marketing Strategy

To start a successful content marketing strategy, you need to think about what types of content your target audience would find valuable. This includes both, the type of content and where you plan on posting it.

To make the most of your content marketing efforts, you'll want to create different types of content for different channels like your website, blog, social media, or email.

Here are a few ideas for different types of content you can include in your content marketing strategy,

Blog posts: A blog is a perfect place to start your content

marketing strategy. Blog posts are easy to create and publish, and they can address a variety of topics that are relevant to your business.

Ebooks: An ebook is a great way to compile your best content on one specific topic into a single resource that your audience can easily refer to.

Videos: Video is becoming a more and more popular way to create and publish content. You can use videos to share your story or provide helpful tips on a variety of topics.

Infographics: Visual content is a great way to break through the noise and really catch your audience's attention. Infographics are particularly useful for sharing statistics or graphs.

Podcasts: Podcasts are an excellent content marketing tool because they allow you to host a regular show where you can discuss your industry and attract new customers.

Once you've created content, it's time to implement your content marketing strategy. You can't just publish new content and hope for the best; you need to promote it for your strategy to work.

Here are a few ways to promote your content marketing strategy,

Identify your channels: Decide where you want to publish your content. You might want to start with your website or social media channels.

Schedule your posts: You need to publish new content carefully. You need to make sure you publish posts at the right times for the right people.

Pick your topics: You don't have to create new content on every possible topic. Instead, you can create an editorial calendar based on a few key topics.

Measure your results: Once you start publishing content, it's important to track how well it performs. This will help you make adjustments as needed.

Content marketing is a highly effective way to get your brand in front of new customers and build trust with your existing customers.

As a marketer, your goal is to create engaging and valuable content that solves your audience's problems and helps your brand stand out from the competition.

To do this, you need to understand your audience and what topics they're interested in. Once you know this information, it's time to create and distribute your content. You can do this on your website, social media channels, podcast, or any other type of online channel.

ANOTHER BONUS

Consultation Call.

As a business consultant, I understand the challenges faced by businesses in terms of business development, systems optimization, and marketing strategies. I delve into the pain points and gaps that hinder growth and success. By conducting a thorough analysis of the business landscape, market dynamics, and industry trends, I gain insights into the specific problems my clients face.

My unique approach sets me apart from other consultants. I emphasize a holistic approach, offering customized solutions tailored to the individual needs of each client. With my proven expertise and experience, I bring a valuable perspective to help businesses succeed.

Through my approach, I offer tangible solutions to businesses. If you are seeking guidance on solving your business problems and growing your business to new heights, I invite you to book a consultation call with me.

To book a consultation call, please go to - https://rcl.ink/krf5P

I look forward to support your business in achieving its full potential.

ABOUT THE AUTHOR

Anuj Sharma

Anuj Sharma, a renowned Serial Entrepreneur, Investor, Consultant, and Digital Marketing Expert. With an unwavering passion for entrepreneurship, Anuj's journey began at a young age, propelling him to refine his skills and achieve remarkable success in multiple ventures.

Driven by a profound desire to uplift and empower business owners, Anuj's collaborative and dynamic approach has earned him a reputation as a problem-solving virtuoso. Boasting an impressive many years of experience, he has become a trusted name in driving business growth and success.

Anuj's expertise in digital marketing is second to none, backed by his certification as a Google advertising expert. This distinction further validates his mastery in leveraging the digital realm to elevate businesses to new heights.

One of Anuj's greatest strengths lies in his ability to unravel complex challenges faced by businesses of all sizes. His strategic thinking and innate problem-solving abilities enable him to provide effective solutions that pave the way for high growth and sustainable success.